The War at Home

A Columbia's Fire Book

THE WAR AT HOME

One Family's Fight Against PTSD

Shawn J. Gourley

Columbia's Fire

The Grumpy Dragon, LLC

Colorado Springs

The War at Home

One Family's Fight Against PTSD

Cover Design: Rose L. Hayden

Cover Photo: Andrew Grammer

Layout/Prepress: Ray Henry

Editor: Spring Lea Henry

Publisher Cataloging-in-Publication Data

Gourley, Shawn J.

The War At Home: One family's fight with PTSD

p. cm.

Includes bibliographical references.

ISBN-10 0-9790084-6-8

ISBN-13 978-0-9790084-6-7

1. Post-traumatic stress disorder -- United States. 2. War -- Psychological aspects. 3. Combat Disorders -- United States. Stress Disorders, Post-Traumatic -- United States. 4. Veterans -- psychology -- United States. 5. Veteran. 6. September 11 Terrorist Attacks, 2001. 7. War on Terrorism, 2001-2009. 8. Marriage. 9. Communication in marriage.

I. Title.

RC552.P67

616.85/21

Columbia's Fire

is an imprint of

The Grumpy Dragon, LLC

1818 Whitman Road

Colorado Springs, CO 80910

www.grumpydragon.com

Library of Congress Control Number: 2011936503

Disclaimers

This book was written and is intended for informational purposes only. This book does not contain or constitute medical advice nor is it an attempt to practice medicine. This book does not establish a doctor-patient relationship between the author and the reader.

The information contained herein is not intended to replace consultation with a qualified medical professional. The information in this book should in no way be considered a specific plan for disease management. Individuals should consult a qualified healthcare provider for medical advice and answers to personal health questions. The reader should follow the treating physicians' advice. No part of this book should be used as the basis of self-diagnosis or treatment, or any other medical decision.

The author makes no warranty to the accuracy, completeness, or timeliness of the information contained in this book. The author of this book expressly disclaims all liability for damages of any kind arising out of use, reference to, or reliance on any information provided in this book.

References in this book to any and all specific products, services or processes do not constitute or imply an endorsement or recommendation by the author.

Links or references to other organizations or websites do not constitute or imply an endorsement or recommendation by the author. Furthermore, the author has no responsibility for the accuracy or content of information provided by these sites or organizations and expressly disclaims all liability for damages of any kind arising out of use, reference to, or reliance on any information provided by outside parties.

Some information about military incidents in this book has been scaled back in detail to avoid presenting information that could potentially reveal sensitive tactics, techniques, and strategies of our national defense and out of concern for our readers who may have PTSD and might be susceptible to being triggered by said details.

This book is dedicated to Justin,
the *Military With PTSD*™ Facebook family,
all veterans, service members, and their families,
and everyone who is affected by PTSD.

Very special thanks go to Soldiers' Angels for all
the support they have given both me and all
military personnel with PTSD.

Acknowledgements

I could not have written this book without the constant support of my husband, Justin. Not only did he give me space and time to work on it and help watch the kids while I was working, but he opened up his heart to put down on the page the raw truth of what he was thinking and feeling during this difficult time in our marriage. I deeply appreciate my kids for their patience while Mommy was working so hard on the book. Justin's step-mom, Paula, was also a big help in getting us to communicate with each other and provided support for our family while I worked on getting the book finished.

I would also like to thank my best friend, LeeAnn, for sticking with me through this storm and doing her best to understand the good person Justin still is, despite the poor actions he took during the thick of our battle with PTSD. I also need to give a big shout out to my friend, Patty, who kept my kids entertained as I raced to finish the book in time to make my deadline.

I would like to thank the whole community on the Military with PTSD™ Facebook Page who helped me come up with the idea for the structure of this book as a dialogue between myself and Justin as well as thinking of a good title for the book and asking lots of questions to help me develop the content. This book would not exist without all of you! From that group, Jennie McFarling, in particular, played a special role in helping me connect with people important not only to this book, but also to all military with PTSD and their families. I also really appreciate the page admins: Jason Hutt, Michelle Smith, Brittney Biddle, Sarah Privitar, and Mollie Moncrief who kept things going while I was distracted with writing and editing this book.

Special thanks to Sarah for also being the one who created the initial cover for the book. I need to thank Andrew Grammer for the cover photo and Cindy Brown for making a video for the book. Thanks to Rose Hayden for creating the final jacket design. Also thanks go to Charisa A. Harmon for helping me create the legal disclaimer and Mary Beth Cottingham and Patricia Douglas for helping me edit the much shorter free version of this book that started it all.

There's a long list of movers and shakers who should be thanked for all the energy they put into this book. For starters, Carl Cronk not only helped me connect with some important people but also worked hard to provide vet support for people on the Facebook group. Bob Calvert and GI Wayne were both kind enough to invite me for radio interviews. Jamie Reno was instrumental in the early publicity for the free mini-book by granting me an interview on the Home Post website for Military in San Diego about the Facebook page and all the help we're providing there. Sandra L. Gruber from Citizens Soldiers, Inc. and Max Reinhardt were both instrumental in getting the word out, as well as Max Harris who also let me write as a guest on his blog. Cari Johnson helped connect me with other important voices in the PTSD support community.

Marshēle Carter Waddell and Dr. Janet J. Seahorn, PhD, both who have books of their own on PTSD, were extremely supportive during the entire process, and Patricia Evans gave me some great professional advice about how to handle psychological issues in a book like this.

I would like to thank Anna Faulk, Michelle Jackson, and Laura Hoeppner for volunteering to be critical civilian readers to make sure my book would be understood by people unfamiliar with either military life or PTSD.

This list wouldn't be complete without acknowledging other members from the veteran support community, Anthony Farina, Boone Cutler, Soldier-Hard The Voice, Sgt. Leo Dunson, and the members of Soldiers' Angels, Blue Star Mothers, FamilyofaVet.com, and Citizen Soldiers, Inc.

This book could not have happened if Dave Kashmer had not introduced me to "his friend, the editor." I owe extreme gratitude to Tracey Firestone, Curtis Folts, Cindy McGuire, and Dori Eppstein-Ransom for being absolutely indispensable copy-editors. You all did exceptional work on very tight deadlines, and I cannot thank you enough!

Lastly, a special thank you to my editor and publisher, Spring Lea Henry, who gave me a chance to tell my story without changing it, for helping me make this book better than I ever thought it could be, and for keeping me laughing the whole time.

— Shawn J. Gourley

Table of Contents

Introduction

She didn't have to wear a uniform or carry heavy combat gear or travel to Iraq with a battle mind mentality. She wasn't exposed to loud blasts and explosions. She wasn't in a far away war-torn country held up in a restricted space for days at a time with the same people without modern conveniences. She wasn't sent on a special mission for her country knowing she might not come home. Yet, she was presented with a different and unexpected mission for which there was no training, no instructions, no supervision, no yellow ribbons, no medals.

So it is that the author of this timely book—a bright, feisty, yet vulnerable young woman—has written (and lived) The War at Home. She has poured her heart and soul into the pages you are about to read and devoted herself to helping others who have post-traumatic stress disorder (PTSD) and those who love them and often carry the burden of fighting "the war at home" alone. Shawn and her husband, Justin, tell their own story. To their credit, they have been reaching out trying to help others and have provided a forum to connect, exchange ideas and resources, and carve a small place in society and today's social media for networking and positive self-help solutions for returning veterans with issues and spouses who must cope as well. With this book, there is now a chance that their story will raise awareness in those unfamiliar with the rigors of a life with PTSD.

War—with its heroes, survivors and casualties—is not real to those who do not live it. What is it like for a returning war veteran who carries the invisible wounds of war to try to fit in again when nothing will ever be the same? What does it take to live with the toll of the war experience? You will have a personal glimpse into the lives and struggles of one such couple in the chapters that follow.

Personal stories like these are necessary to our education about PTSD. The emotional and mental effects of deployment to a dangerous far-away land, though well documented, continue to be researched, and each case study adds new information. Resiliency of many service members is remarkable following deployments. Exposure to trauma beyond the realm of normal experience is a human condition of displacement, anger, suffering, and feeling misunderstood. Developing an understanding of PTSD will help us understand more about the human condition as a whole.

Healing the invisible wounds of trauma and danger are never easy. They run as deep as one's own soul. PTSD was felt in silence or loud agony long before the Diagnostic Statistical Manual of Mental Disorders gave it credibility and psychiatric definition. Post-deployment problems of depression, adjustment reactions, and substance abuse occurred long before yellow ribbon events and the wars of this generation. World War II veterans with combat related issues did not talk about what they had seen and survived. Many who could not cope with total stoicism became chronic alcoholics. The Vietnam veteran was deprived of everything he earned including respect and even a "Welcome

Home." If PTSD manifested itself in those exposed to horrific events, it often yielded itself to drug addiction as a form of misguided self-medication for brutal and dehumanizing flashbacks and triggers. While PTSD can never be an excuse to commit a crime, making appropriate services available can certainly be a deterrent.

Traumatic brain injury (TBI) has been called the signature wound of Operation Iraqi Freedom and Operation Enduring Freedom. Despite efforts to screen, it is believed some come home with this neurological injury and subsequent cognitive changes but are not diagnosed. Almost 20% of veterans returning from Iraq and Afghanistan exhibit positive symptoms for PTSD and clinical depression according to a well-received 2008 RAND study. Most combat veterans return changed but strong, even with adjustment issues which subside in about a year. However, many return with one, two, or even three of these clinical mental health syndromes. The search for psychological tools of survival continues. Available treatments such as Cognitive Behavior Therapy (CBT), Prolonged Exposure Therapy, Eye Movement Desensitization and Reprocessing (EMDR), and psychotropic medications when indicated offer hope to restore quality of life.

Despite this constant search for new methods of treatment, flashbacks and frustrations may linger. The attempts to fit in may be a long and frustrating struggle. The fight to adapt upon return from combat can haunt someone for a lifetime and, without treatment, force them into a cage of invisible isolation. It can destroy marriages and family relationships and diminish the capacity to parent. This is not an acceptable scenario. The Department of Defense has improved its response to provide services through Military One Source, Military Family Life Consultants, and other programs. The VA continues to expand and improve mental health care and substance abuse treatment as well as outreach through Vet Centers and Mobile Vet Centers. Many will still fall through the cracks or feel too stigmatized to seek treatment. Some will visit the gates but have a negative experience and never return.

The suicide rate among returning combat veterans of this generation is a national disgrace and tragedy. It has become the Army's "War Within." Our military has developed impressive suicide prevention programs in response to this frightening increase in suicides. But this will not reach all of those who are troubled. They have taken steps to convince service members it takes courage to seek help. Will this be enough? No, it will not. Our communities must also be supportive as well as grateful to those who have served on our behalf and have given up chunks of their lives. The unnecessary psychological and mental health casualties of war among our citizens and their families will only be reduced when we all help those affected to make peace with themselves and their experiences. Shawn's book is an excellent reminder to us all to keep that gratitude in our hearts... and maybe now and again remember to say, "Thank you for your Service."

Beverly A. Taylor, LCSW

Professional Military Mental Health Service Provider
Military Stress Specialist
Licensed Clinical Social Worker
Daughter of a Vietnam-Era
Veteran and Career Army Officer

List of Terms Used

Arrested Landing: This is a type of landing used on aircraft carriers where the runways are really short. A system of cables catches the plane and halts its motion as it touches down on deck.

ASVAB: The Armed Services Vocational Aptitude Battery (ASVAB) is a test used to determine qualification for enlistment in the U.S. armed forces.

Battle Buddy: In the military, this is a soldier who has gained your trust and who will watch your back when you're in dangerous situations. In casual/civilian use, it means much the same thing.

DSM: *Diagnostic and Statistical Manual of Mental Disorders.* This is a book mental health care professionals use to diagnose conditions of their patients.

Military PTSD: Post-traumatic stress disorder that is caused specifically by events that occur in the service such as witnessing horrific deaths or participating in combat.

OEF: *Operation Enduring Freedom.* This is America's military action in Afghanistan in response to the terrorist attacks of September 11, 2001.

OIF: *Operation Iraqi Freedom.* This is America's military action in Iraq.

PTSD: *Post-traumatic stress disorder.* A collection of behaviors as a result of living through large trauma or series of small traumas over a long period of time. The behaviors include physical, mental, and emotional reactions that are triggered by environmental conditions that remind one of the original trauma.

STSD: *Secondary traumatic stress disorder.* This is a form of PTSD that occurs in the family of a victim of PTSD because the behavior of the person with PTSD is, in and of itself, traumatic to the family. It is not recognized by doctors yet, but therapists are starting to tell their patients about it.

Securing A Body: This means that a member of the security team makes sure that a body in an incident remains untouched until medical personnel arrive. This may include constructing temporary walls/barriers around the body and clearing the area of excess personnel.

VA: *Veterans Affairs.* The US Department of Veteran' Affairs was created to provide patient care and federal benefits to veterans and their dependents.

Vet Center: These are institutions funded by the United States government to provide individual, group, and family counseling to all veterans who served in any combat zone. However, for the family to receive counseling, the veteran has to be active in therapy with the Vet Center.

The War At Home

My children and I did not volunteer to go to war.
How could you not warn me the war
was coming straight into our home?

I had no warning or instruction
as to what to watch out for.
The soldier returned home and not my husband.
I got a little pamphlet explaining that most soldiers
may have to readjust to being home.

I believed you and trusted you
when you said the readjustment period
may take a few months but they should experience
a successful transition back into the home.

Months turned into years,
and every time I would call for help
I was brushed away.

I called for help because my home
had turned into a battlefield.
Guns were being drawn
and my children and I became the enemy.
We lived our life walking on eggshells out of fear.
For almost 5 years we lived in hell.

I had to use every ounce of strength I had
to keep this family together.
My husband proudly served this country
and would gladly do it again if asked.
But when his family needed help,
you allowed them to suffer for years.

We did not want money.
We wanted to have a normal life.
We would have had a chance
if you would have been truthful,
if you would have told these soldiers' families
what to watch out for.
You should have told us about PTSD!

PROLOGUE

September 11, 2001, 7:46 CST.
The North Tower of the World Trade Center is struck by American Airlines Flight 11.

I wake up as usual at 7:45 or so. I start getting ready for work and get my daughter ready for daycare. My life is ticking along to the same old rhythm it always does. As I'm getting ready for work, I turn on the news and see that a plane has crashed into the World Trade Center. I think it must be an accident. The words, "terrorist attack," never even cross my mind.

September 11, 2001, 8:03 CST.
The South Tower of the World Trade Center is struck by United Airlines Flight 175.

I drive my daughter to daycare, and when I arrive, I discover that another plane has struck the World Trade Center. All I can think is, *This is deliberate now.* My friend LeeAnn calls and says that she heard one of the planes was headed to Las Vegas, which is where my parents are flying that very day. I frantically call my parents and wake them up. I didn't know they were already there. Relieved, I go on to work at T.G.I. Friday's. I'm one of the first to arrive and immediately turn on the TV.

September 11, 2001, 8:37 CST.
The Pentagon is struck by American Airlines Flight 77.

As my servers start to arrive, they announce that the Pentagon has been hit by a third plane. By now, I'm feeling angry. I want to know who did this and why our government wasn't able to stop it. Later when I hear that our boys are being dispatched, I feel a sense of vindication. I think, We're going to get 'em.

September 11, 2001, 9:03 CST.
United Airlines Flight 93 crash lands in a field in Pennsylvania.

Still at work, the mall announces we are closing, but someone from corporate on the phone is telling me we won't close for anything. I can't believe I'm standing here arguing something so stupid when America is under attack like this. I know he must be feeling just as confused as the rest of us about what's right to do, but to me the answer is obvious. I finally convince him we're closing and go forward into my day trying to deal with mundane life in unbelievable circumstances. There's an incredible line at the gas pump. One of my servers calls to say her brother is heading for New York. The TV unfolds more horrors by the moment. Church is held on a Tuesday night.

What had happened to my world?

I don't know it yet, but that isn't the question I should be asking myself. The question I should be asking is, "What happens next?" I have no idea how profoundly that day is going to affect the rest of my life.

PROTECTOR

December 1987 — June 2004

Shawn

Justin and I met when he was six and I was ten. He played on my brother's basketball team, and then I became his babysitter. Go ahead and laugh; it's alright.

One night during a storm, there was a strange noise coming from the basement. Even though I was older, it was Justin who took off downstairs with a baseball bat to check out the noise and make sure I was safe. So Justin and I have known each other since we were kids. And we stayed in contact until I went to high school. At that point the age factor came into play. I mean he was in the 7th grade when I was a senior in high school. We didn't resume contact until Justin was already in the Navy.

Justin entered the service in June 2000. He attended boot camp in Chicago and then received orders to the aircraft carrier USS George Washington, CVN-73, as a Machinist Mate. He was assigned to this position because his ASVAB test scores showed his mechanical aptitude was higher than anything else.

Justin's first year in the military was uneventful until September 11, 2001. He had cross-rated to Operation's Specialist, which meant he watched the radar for anything and everything on the water surface. When the attacks on the United States happened on that day, he was in the control room of the USS George Washington. He heard everything that was going on and what orders were being given at that time.

Justin came home to Evansville, IN, for Christmas break December of 2001, and while shopping with his brothers for Christmas gifts he came to TGI Friday's where I was a waitress. It was funny to see Justin all grown up, but it didn't take me long to realize that it was the same old Justin. He was just as sweet and friendly as ever, and he had his same old goofy ways that made me laugh. From that point on we were inseparable.

We talked every chance we got, we e-mailed, and he would come home whenever he could swing a few days off. Justin was great with my daughter, he treated me with the utmost respect, and he was just a fun guy to be around, although at that point in my life I didn't think I wanted a boyfriend. I hadn't had much luck in the past with relationships, so I had decided to focus on me and my daughter. I was one of those strong independent women. I was a single parent, had my own apartment, and had a good job. I thought I had my life headed in the right direction and really didn't think I had the time, or room in my life for a man.

But I quickly found I just couldn't help wanting

to be around him. He was everything I had always dreamed about my future husband being when I was growing up. He was tall, about 6' at least! He was very slender, and though I wished he had a little more meat on him, he was still very attractive to me. Though I loved looking in his blue eyes with long eyelashes, he wouldn't make good eye contact with me because that's what the military taught him to do. In the service, it's considered disrespectful. But he was very sweet and attentive to me, such as always holding doors for me. I didn't have to carry anything, either, which made my heart melt. What more could I ask for?

However, I did make sure our relationship did not get very physical. Experience had taught me that women have sex to get love and men say, "I love you," to get sex, but when a girl gets the sex before the love, she could easily wind up a single mother like I had twice before. Sex confused things, and if I was going to get into a serious relationship, I wanted to make sure it was for the right reasons, not because we had sex and had a physical attraction. So for the first 6 months we dated, I barely allowed Justin to kiss me. Don't get me wrong, resisting him was the hardest thing I had ever done, especially right before he was deployed.

Justin

Yes, Shawn was my babysitter when I was younger and I have always felt this need to protect her. We lost contact until I was in the Navy and came home on leave for Christmas one year. It was so good to see her again, and, believe me, I was instantly attracted to her!

We decided to hang out that night and catch up. I went and bought the *Coyote Ugly* DVD because I overheard her talking about it with some other waitress and saying that she would love to see it. I then stopped and got us some dinner before heading over to her apartment. Hanging out with her was so much fun, and watching her with her daughter was amazing.

I really liked Shawn and wanted to impress her, so before I left that night I took out a twenty, gave it to her, and told her to get her daughter something. Talk about stupid! I don't know what I was thinking. That had to be the worst and goofiest move ever. But it didn't go too bad because Shawn and I saw each other every day for the rest of my leave. I would go to her work, sit in her section, and wait for her to get off work just so I could hang out with her that night.

The first few months, I would drive back to Indiana anytime I had a weekend off. I would drive 12 hours one way after I got off work and then, two days later, drive 12 hours back to Norfolk. I would take her out, and she loved it that I would open doors for her and treated her like a queen. It didn't take long for us to realize that there was much more than friendship between us.

To me, Shawn looked exactly like Betty Boop, and that was what I started calling her sometimes as a pet name. She was short, only 4'9", but she had a really curvy body. She had really big breasts and very muscular thighs, both of which were a turn-on to me. She had a really thin waist, blonde hair, and brown eyes. I kind of wished she had a different color of eyes, but the rest of her was so attractive to me it didn't matter much.

On one of our dates, Shawn and I went back to T.G.I. Friday's to have a few drinks before heading home. Shawn went to go talk to some of her co-workers, and from across the bar I heard her say, "I'm going to marry this man whether he realizes it or not." I didn't know if she really meant that or if it was the alcohol talking. I think Shawn thought since she was across the bar I wouldn't be able to hear what she said.

I knew I had a six month tour coming up, and I really hoped she would wait for me until I came home. I knew that she may not, and I would have to be okay with that if that was her choice. Shawn was sending me mixed signals, too. She would barely kiss me and always made sure we were never alone together to avoid possible physical contact. I couldn't make heads or tails of her or us. So I left for deployment not exactly sure where we stood.

I found though, that while I was away, I couldn't stop thinking about her. For the first time ever I was thinking about the future and couldn't imagine Shawn and her daughter not being in my life. I had to tell her that, so I wrote her a letter telling her that I wanted to spend the rest of my life with her.

When I reached the port in Greece, I called her hoping she got my letter and was waiting for me, but she didn't answer the phone. So I called my mom and asked if she had seen or talked to Shawn. My mom then told me that she had seen Shawn one night at TGI Friday's having dinner with another guy. I couldn't believe it. I really thought I had found "The One." I picked up the phone and dialed Shawn's number again. I didn't know what I wanted to accomplish by calling her, but I wanted to at least talk to her and tell her to ignore my letter. When she answered the phone and realized it was me she said, "Mr. Gourley, are you telling me I should start planning our wedding?"

"What? Are you serious?" *Yes!* She did love me and wanted to be with me.

I was so excited I could barely talk, but I managed to tell her that I had been temporarily assigned to the Military Police and thought with my training when I came home that I should be able to get a job as a cop. I had it all planned out and was going to stay as an MP because I really liked it.

Shawn

In June 2002, the USS George Washington was deployed to support Operation Enduring Freedom (OEF) in the Middle East and Arabian Gulf. As much as I liked Justin, I wasn't sure that our relationship would withstand his Naval deployments, not because I wouldn't wait for him, but more because he was young, was going to be gone for 6 months at a time when deployed, and would live 12 hours away when he was back in the United States. Those are not exactly the best conditions to try to make a serious relationship work. But then I thought about how sweet he was and how well he treated my daughter. He made me smile, he made me laugh, and most of all with the way he treated me, I felt like I had found my Prince Charming.

I tried as best as I could not to worry about what might or might not happen. Only time would tell what would happen between us, so I busied myself with work and my daughter.

I ran into his mother one night at work while I was eating dinner with a co-worker. I asked her if she had heard from Justin and how he was doing. She said he sent her emails and that he was fine. I told her to let him know I said hi the next time she talked to him, she told me she would, and we left it at that.

I was completely shocked the next day when I opened my mailbox and there was a letter from Justin in there. I hadn't heard anything in two months from him, so I assumed he wasn't as interested in me as I thought he was. I was shocked again when I read his letter. He was crazy about me, and this time I knew it was real. While reading the letter, I knew I was going to be getting married to this man. In the letter he told me he would call me at his next port, and if I didn't return the feelings, he would understand.

So every day I would reread the letter and practice what I would say to him when he called. I had it all planned out. But when he called, I freaked and didn't know what to say other than to ask if I should I start planning our wedding. Hearing his excitement to what I said put me on cloud nine, so as soon as we got off the phone, I ran and picked up some bridal magazines to start getting some ideas for the wedding.

Justin

I still had 4 months left on the tour that I was on at the time. It seemed to go by pretty fast, which was a good thing, because seeing Shawn again was all I could think about.

I couldn't wait to come home, and during our first tour in support of OEF we saw absolutely no action. Everything was good. I had nothing but the future to look forward to.

On October 2, 2002, while on our way back home, the band 3 Doors Down performed on our ship. It was a huge and amazing concert. They even used footage of the concert aboard our ship for the video "When I'm Gone." I had to work security during the concert, so I didn't get to enjoy it as other crew members did. I was still able to hear the music and then later got to meet the band and get an autographed CD.

Shawn

On February 4, 2003, while running carrier qualifications back home, the USS George Washington responded to a distress call from the Coast Guard. Four survivors were rescued, and one person died of hypothermia. The small fishing vessel they were on had caught fire. Justin was responsible for securing the body of the deceased while the other four were treated on board the USS George Washington. This was the first time Justin had ever handled a dead body.

When he called me to tell me about what had happened, the first thing I asked him was if he was all right. His response was, "Well yeah, why wouldn't I be? It's part of life. No reason to dwell on it." So I dropped it.

Justin

As soon as I got back to the states, I went home for Valentine's Day to propose to Shawn. She was still at work, so I went back to her apartment and made us a nice dinner. I wanted everything to be perfect for this night. Problem is, when Shawn came home from work, she asked me to leave. She told me she didn't care where I went, just so long as it wasn't at her apartment for the next 30 minutes or so.

What could I do? She was just flat out kicking me out. She knew dinner was ready and acted like she didn't even see it. So I left and went for a drive. I knew what was coming next: She didn't want me or had found someone else. So after about 15 minutes of driving around, I decided to go talk to my step-dad. He would tell me exactly what he thought was going on.

But he wasn't any help. All he said was, "Women: if you can figure them out you'll be the luckiest man in the world."

So then I called my mom who told me not to worry. She said Shawn probably wanted to get all cleaned up and make herself pretty for me. So I decided to head back to the apartment and see what was going on.

When I got there the door was locked so I had to knock. When Shawn opened the door, I about fell over. She was wearing this tight, low cut, white, button-up shirt and a plaid mini-skirt. She had put on make-up, and her hair was down and curled. She was *Hot* with a capital H! I walked in; Shawn shut the door and then grabbed me and kissed me hard. It was hot! When I kissed her, I knew there was no other girl for me. So I got down on one knee and asked her to marry me.

Of course she said yes, and over the next few days we started telling everyone. Our friends and family all commented on how happy we were together. Even my step-dad made the comment, "People aren't as happy as the two of you are. It's not normal, but I guess that means you found 'The One.' Good for you!" See?!? I knew I was right about this girl.

Shawn

In the past I have always hated Valentine's Day. It seemed like I was always left crying on that day, so I learned that if I didn't have any expectations, I wouldn't get my feelings hurt.

When I got home from work, I could see the table and candles and knew he had gone out of his way to make this Valentine's Day very special for me. I wanted to do something in return for Justin, and the only thing I could think of was to fix myself up for him. But I wanted to surprise him, so I asked him to leave without any explanation.

I'm a jeans and t-shirt, hair in a ponytail, no make-up kinda girl, so I wanted to go the extra mile for him. I picked out a button up shirt and skirt since I don't ever wear things like that.

When Justin came back home, I grabbed him and kissed him to show him how much I appreciated him making this Valentine's Day very special and to let him know how much I loved him. When he got down on one knee, I was stunned. *So that's what this is all about! I thought it was for Valentine's Day.*

We started planning our wedding which was going to be on September 11, 2003. I told Justin I wanted a big wedding in the church that I attended. I also informed him at that time, before we got married in my church we would have to do marriage counseling. I could tell he wasn't overly thrilled with having to attend, but he told me he would do it so that I could have my church wedding.

We went to the church and spoke with the musical director who would also be our counselor and the one conducting the ceremony. He gave us each a workbook called *Preparing for Marriage.* With Justin not living in Evansville, we would have to do counseling when he would come to visit instead of the 6 weeks it would normally take. We decided to go ahead and do session one later that week before Justin had to return to Norfolk, VA.

We both worked on the questions in session one, which focused on helping both of us understand what expectations we were bringing into the marriage. It also had a project that would offer us insight, wisdom, and advice from someone who knew us best. So I chose to ask my best friend

LeeAnn those questions. She pointed out my strengths that she thought would help me in marriage and also my weaknesses that she felt I needed to work on overcoming. But it was her advice for keeping a happy marriage that hit me the hardest and really stuck with me.

"Love is a choice, not a feeling. Remember you *chose* to love him, because it won't always feel good! Keep lines of communication open; the silent treatment is cruel.

"When it comes to sex, be open and honest; men don't know how to read minds.

"Never threaten to leave; stay strong in your commitment."

I would return to this advice time and again when things got bad.

When it was time for him to leave, we decided that I would take a vacation in March and come visit him in Norfolk, Virginia.

In March 2003, Justin had to attend an anti-terrorism training course for one week where he learned different types of terrorist tactics, ran mock terrorist drills, and was certified on many different weapons.

I arrived in Virginia right after this training course was completed. Justin told me that our September wedding was not possible because they were unsure when they were going to be deployed again. This left us only two options: elope or wait until Justin was out of the military. So, of course, we eloped.

The day we got married I was so happy and proud that he had made me his wife. I wanted to take him straight back to the hotel room and consummate our marriage. I am a woman, and this moment was something I had looked forward to my whole life. I figured he would be just as excited being that I had held him off for so long. It didn't work out that way though, in fact it was a disaster.

It seemed as though he was going through the motions and wasn't as excited as I was about making love to his new wife. Okay, maybe the fact that the maid walked in and interrupted us did not help matters at all, but I figured it would be something he could shake off. I just remember thinking, *Okay, maybe this time didn't go as planned, but it will get better.*

I didn't realize at the time what a big deal the maid walking in on us was to Justin. When she opened the door, I sprang up out of the bed and ran into the bathroom, leaving Justin to deal with it alone. Not only had I left him alone in a social situation, but it was an awkward one. I didn't know how uncomfortable he felt, and he never said a word, but I thought about it later when Justin started changing.

As the week went on while I was in Virginia, I could tell something else was wrong with Justin, but I couldn't figure out what. He just didn't seem to be himself. He was very tense, distant, and serious. I asked him what the hell had happened in that training course. His reply was, "Nothing. I just have a lot more stress in my position now."

I was not content with that answer, so I kept asking him, "What did you learn? What did you do? What did you see?"

Justin told me about how in the classroom they talked about what happened to the USS Cole and watched a lot of videos showing the aftermath. They taught them about how easy it is for terrorists to sneak bombs into just about anywhere and how they use children as bombs. They were taught to see themselves as "expendable assets" or, in other words, cannon fodder. The U.S. had the right to use them in any way they saw fit in order to defend national security. He also talked about his weapon qualifications and how well he'd done on the sniper test. And he told me that he got promoted to Rapid Response Team Leader.

Sitting there talking to him gave me the chills. There was no emotion in his voice, and his eyes were black as the night. The fun-loving Justin I knew my whole life had been transformed into a well-trained, highly-skilled machine that could kill without thinking twice.

Before I left, he assured me that things would get better once he got used to the new position. And for a few months, things were a little bit better. In June 2003 we bought our first house together, and Justin came home any chance he got to help me. It was a project house, and we knew it needed some work when we bought it.

We had Justin's paycheck directed back to Evansville so I could pay the bills and fix up the house. We tried to do most of the work ourselves to cut costs and hopefully start saving money to fall back on.

What problems or disagreements we did have I wrote off to Justin being exhausted from driving 12 hours home and then 12 hours back to Norfolk every other weekend. Plus, we were newlyweds and trying to get used to being married.

Justin

When I returned to Norfolk in March, 2003, I was sent to an anti-terrorism training school to enhance my training as a security officer. This was the same training as the anti-terrorist force protection team was receiving. My job was no longer just to be a Navy MP, it was now focused on protecting DoD high-value assets, such as ships, cargo, and people, against terrorist attacks at sea. Once there my eyes were opened, and my sense of being safe quickly disappeared. I realized how serious this was and how quickly your life could end if you didn't stay alert and always watch for danger.

A recent suicide bombing of one our Naval vessels was programmed into our heads. A small boat pulled up next to the USS Cole at a refueling stop, and the terrorists on the boat even waved or saluted the crew members on the ship. The crew did not see them to be a threat as they approached, and the only two members on security patrol had weapons that were not loaded. The craft that approached them looked like one of the boats that helped guide them into port to be refueled. So everyone on board the USS Cole was caught unaware. It was drilled into my head over and over again, *Be ready for anything, and be ready for these types of terrorist attacks.*

After this attack, the Navy put in place parameters that created a force protection zone. This is the space that surrounds a ship, when a boat enters that space, they are in the kill zone. It made us all a little edgier when we were on guard because we had to be on alert all the time and notice everyone and everything around us. We were taught that if you let your guard down even for a second, you're dead.

Also at the anti-terrorism training course, they taught us how a terrorist can make a bomb out of things that you would never expect, including everyday ordinary objects. We learned about how they would use women and children to sneak bombs past security. We ran drill after drill until we stopped hesitating and acting on emotion when it came to doing what was needed.

Everything I thought I knew and thought about people changed then. No one could be trusted. My view on life now was simple: *Everyone was the enemy because you never really knew who the enemy was.*

I took my training very seriously and at the end of the class I was promoted to Rapid Response Team Leader. The Rapid Response Team is like the Navy's version of SWAT. It was my responsibility to ensure that the Security Officers on the USS George Washington were trained, ready to respond to anything, and completed each task without incident.

When I was finished with training, Shawn and I got married. That week, which should have been happy, was a nightmare. From my view, Shawn was emotional, clingy, and sex-crazed. She took everything so personally and then would start crying. I was thinking, *What the hell? I marry her, and now she does this?*

She kept asking about the training, and so I finally laid it out for her. I told her what we did, and I explained to her my job had changed and was more stressful now. I also explained that we were down in Virginia where I worked every day, and I couldn't just shut this mode off. She looked at me like I was crazy. I knew I couldn't get her to understand, so I told her just to give me some time and things would get better once I got used to this position. And it seemed to level her out for a little while.

Things continued on and we bought a house a few months later. I found out I would have one last tour to the Middle East, and we would be leaving in January 2004. So some things would have to be changed as far as money so we could pay the house payment and bills.

We changed my check deposits to our account in Indiana, and I got about $100 every pay check for myself. I felt like I didn't need any more money than that since I was deployed. We moved into the house in June, and the next few months got a little crazy, but that was nothing compared to what was getting ready to happen on our ship.

Shawn

On September 11, 2003, on Justin's ship, an F-18 made an arrested landing, which uses a cabling system to stop a plane when it is landing on the deck of an aircraft carrier. However, the cable broke, sending the plane crashing into the water. The pilot was able to eject and wasn't hurt, but the arresting gear cable snapped back across the deck of the USS George Washington, injuring several crew members. Justin had to secure the area where the injured crew members would be treated and assist in keeping them calm.

He emailed me to let me know what happened, and we talked about it. You know how guys are; they are supposed to be strong, like nothing is ever a big deal. But I knew Justin better than he knew himself, I think. I could tell he was pretty shaken up from the whole ordeal. It was all he talked about for days, even though he would blow me off and tell me things like, "It happens," or, "People die; it's part of life." So I decided the next time he came home we were going to do something fun for the weekend to help get his mind off of things.

In October when he came home, we went down to his dad's river camp for the weekend for a cookout and to go 4-wheeling with his dad and step-mom. We had such a fun time and maybe a little too much to drink, but, hey, we're adults! The only problem with having too much to drink is you tend to forget about precautions to avoid getting pregnant. Sure enough, that is exactly what happened, though I didn't know it at the time.

Then in November 2003, one of the airmen was killed while working on an airplane. Justin once again had to secure the body and the area until the investigation was complete before anyone else could "tag and bag" the body. He emailed me again to tell me about it. Just like the previous times with him, it was no big deal. It was another one of those things that "just happened." I tried to get him to talk about it more this time, but he wouldn't. It was like he wanted to pretend it never happened. But I wasn't a counselor, and I figured if he wanted to talk about things he would. Plus, through an email it was hard to tell how he was really feeling. It wasn't like I could hear his voice and be able to tell if he was being honest about things or not.

Justin

I will never forget the day that the mass casualty alarm rang out across our ship. It was one of those alarms you hoped you would never hear. But that day a plane had crashed while making its landing, and the arresting cable snapped back across the deck. I immediately ran up to the flight deck and started making routes and blocking off areas so the injured could be treated. At that point, I wouldn't have let the President himself through if he wanted past. I didn't care who you were; no one was getting past me unless they were medics or injured. I then had to help keep the injured crew members calm. I had to tell them they would be alright, even if I didn't think they were.

When it was over, I couldn't get the whole thing out of my head, but everyone kept asking me if I was okay. Then they asked me what got into me. I know I am usually a quiet guy that most people wouldn't notice, but I did my job and couldn't let emotions come into play. What was so strange about that? I just wanted to forget it happened, but when I closed my eyes I could see it again. And each time more and more people were injured. I couldn't help them all. This was crazy! I had to get my head straight. So when we returned from our trials I took a few days to go back home.

The break was nice, and it helped a lot. When I got back to the ship, I was focused and ready to go. But then a month later a crew member on the ship was killed when a fuel tank fell from the belly of the plane he was working on and crushed him. I was in charge so I had to secure the body and keep people away. I had my team build a wall so no one could see when they lifted the fuel tank and his body was exposed. To see him after they removed the fuel tank shook me to my core. This was a shipmate who I saw and talked to every day, and there was no way I could even recognize him anymore. It was hard to imagine that someone was there one day and gone the next. I thought about the fishing boat we rescued and the body of the one person who died that I had to secure. Then I thought about the plane crash and I realized that at any moment it could be any of us laying here dead.

If everything happening on the ship wasn't enough, I then found out Shawn was pregnant, which was the last thing we needed. Shawn was trying to fix up the house, so she wasn't saving any money. I found that out from my step-dad who told me how she was blowing every bit of money that I earned. This made me angry. I had no control over what was happening and no say on anything. I felt like my life was spiraling out of control.

Shawn

Shortly after that, I found out I was pregnant and thought Justin would be so excited that he was going to be a dad. Boy was I ever wrong! When I told him I was pregnant through email, he wrote back and asked, "What? You're kidding, right?" When I told him no, he messaged me back with, "Well that's just great." I thought if I gave it time, he would come around. When he came home for Christmas, I thought we'd do things to get ready for the baby, but instead we spent most of the time fighting.

I hated that we were fighting like that, especially since he was getting ready to be deployed again. So when I drove Justin back to Norfolk, I tried to make the best of the long drive and not do or say anything that might upset him again. But then he really surprised me and started to talk to me about why he was so stressed.

He explained to me that in his position, he couldn't relax and that things had to be run in a particular order. As security on the USS George Washington, he couldn't let his guard down for one moment. I acknowledged what he was saying, but tried to explain to him that our home was not the ship. He then flew into a rage, going on about the USS Cole and how the ship's safety was his responsibility and that his training was not a light switch that could be turned on and off.

The last thing I said to him when he got out of my car was, "I can't wait until you're out of the military so I can have the man I married back."

In January 2004, the USS George Washington was again sent to the Middle East and Arabian Gulf in support of Operation Iraqi Freedom (OIF) and Operation Enduring Freedom (OEF). This would be Justin's last deployment, and his military career would end in June 2004.

But on his last tour, while making the transit through the Suez Canal, there was an incident involving a boat headed straight towards the USS George Washington during Justin's watch. This event, along with the plane crash and dead bodies, was too much for Justin to handle. PTSD was here.

Justin

I returned home to Shawn one last time during Christmas knowing I was going to be deployed the first week in January. I just wanted to relax and rest, and she just kept on about shopping for the baby and wanting to be intimate. When I told her I didn't want to do any of that, she got all emotional and started crying and saying I didn't love her and didn't want the baby.

I tried to tell her it wasn't that, but she wasn't listening to me. Damn it, why couldn't she see the bigger picture? People were getting seriously hurt and dying, and we weren't even in the war zone yet! I needed to relax at home so I could get ready to go over where people want nothing more than to kill you. I couldn't turn my training off and on. I knew once I was out of the military things would be different, but she couldn't understand, so I ended up leaving with both of us upset. I hated that we left each other that way, but I was focused on being deployed. Her feelings couldn't affect me. I couldn't afford any distractions.

The next week we left Norfolk Virginia and headed for the Middle East to support OIF/OEF campaigns. I thought about our last deployment and really hoped this deployment would go just as smooth, but that hope quickly disappeared while we were making our transit through the Suez Canal.

I was on watch when I noticed a small boat heading straight for us. I called it in to the bridge and was told to keep watch on the boat. So I never took my eyes off of it, all the while thinking about my training and about what happened to the USS Cole.

They were still coming, so I locked and loaded. I took aim at the boat and called the bridge again asking for the go ahead to fire a warning shot. I was told to stand my ground and keep watching them.

"This is ridiculous! What are we going to let them do? Let them get up right next to us so they can blow a hole in the side of this ship?" I said to myself. "No way. Not today. Not on my watch. I'm not gonna die. This isn't going to be a repeat of the Cole."

I stopped talking out loud to myself to call the bridge again and request permission to fire a warning shot. I was told not to make a move until they made a hostile act or I could see the whites of their eyes. I responded by informing them that the boat was almost to the kill zone. As I waited for a reply, I decided if they crossed into the kill zone I was going to fire with or without orders. My heart was pounding; I had never been so scared and pumped up at the same time in my life.

Finally as the bridge responded, I watched the boat suddenly change directions. I informed the bridge of the change in direction and fell back into the chair. That one was too close! I could actually see myself as one of the injured like in the plane crash or one of the dead bodies lying there that I had to secure. I was done. I thought, *Once I am home and outta here, all this will stop.*

So from that day on, the countdown to my release from the military had begun. In June, I was flown off the USS George Washington and headed to Norfolk to be processed out of the military. They did a PTSD evaluation on me, but no way was I going to say I was having problems. I wasn't crazy, and I knew all of this would go away once I got home and got my life started away from all the craziness.

RETURN

June 2004 — September 2004

Shawn

Justin returned home June 2004. I was so excited to have him home. Our baby was due within the next few weeks, and I was ready to settle down into married life. Little did I know this was the beginning of what would be a long nightmare.

Justin brought home two books that he was given before he returned. One was *Coming Home* by Sid Jacobson and Ernie Colon. The other book was *The War Within, One More Step at a Time*, a Doonesbury Book by G.B. Trudeau. Neither book seemed to fit since Justin wasn't in combat nor had received any physical injuries. So I flipped through them but didn't think twice about what they were saying.

I expected it to take a little time for Justin to get used to not being in the military and to readjust to civilian life. I mean, he went from someone telling him what to do and where to be, to having a wife, a step-daughter, and a baby due any time. But I was also concerned because we had never lived together before. I had been responsible for everything on my own. I paid the bills, took care of the kids, and fixed up the house, and I was used to doing it all my way. I wasn't used to having to answer to someone. I wasn't sure what to expect when he got home. Was he going to have me continue to handle everything, or was he going to come back and want to take over everything? As excited as I was, I was nervous about him coming home. But I knew I missed my husband too much to continue being away from him any longer.

I guess the first thing I noticed was that any form of intimacy was nonexistent. Just trying to hold hands or asking him to give me a kiss almost always would turn into a fight. And anything beyond that was out of the question. I was left feeling very alone and confused. We had not seen each other in 6 months, and he was not interested at all in having sex.

When Justin returned home I couldn't wait to start our *real* life as a married couple. I had this perfect reunion already planned out in my head. To me that meant that I would get back the Prince Charming I had dated, not that jerk I married. During his long deployment, all I thought about was what it would be like when he came home. Add being 8 months pregnant to the list, and I was a walking ball of hormones. So believe me, I was shocked when Justin didn't want to have sex. I was a woman and pregnant. What do you expect? I mean, since I now only had part-time custody of my daughter, it meant we had the house to ourselves, but that didn't seem to make a difference. Not only that, but Justin had switched from calling me Betty Boop, which was cute and sexy, to Oompa Loompa because of my baby weight. I took it very personally, and my feelings were hurt.

A few weeks after his return home, our daughter, Jesse, was born. I remember his face, and for a brief few days thought I had my husband back. He was such a proud dad and a very good father. He seemed to know all her little quirks right off the bat like, somehow he knew that the best way to calm her down was to lay her across his lap and rub her back. He helped with putting her down at night, calmed her down if she cried in the middle of the night, and was all smiles. I figured it was time to return home and get our life started. But all that, too, would disappear very quickly.

Once we were back home and getting settled in, Justin started saying he didn't feel well after eating. He'd always have to go lay down because he felt nauseous. At first I wasn't sure if he was telling the truth or if he was just using it as an excuse to get out of doing stuff. But soon I could tell that he really wasn't feeling well.

When I started to unpack Justin's bags, he flipped out. He sternly told me to leave it alone, that he'd get it. I didn't understand what was going on and kept telling him that this was his home and he didn't have to live out of his bag any more. It would be two months before I was able to fully unpack his bags.

Justin

With one bag and a plane ticket home, I eagerly got on the plane. In my mind, I already had everything worked out, what it was going to be like when I got home. But all of that changed on the flight home. President Reagan's funeral was going on in Washington, D.C., so we were stalled in the air for an hour, which caused me to miss my connecting flight.

There was not another flight until the next morning, so instead of being home I had to spend the night in an airport. Needless to say, I was not a happy person at all that night. I just wanted to be home. The next morning I caught the flight and arrived home 18 hours late. Because of the delay only Shawn and my step-dad were at the airport to meet me, not the big welcome home I was expecting. But that wasn't going to get me down. I was still home.

I quickly realized that home was not what I thought it would be. For 4 years I was told what to do and when to do it. I wanted to take a few weeks and relax but I quickly found that wasn't a possibility. I had to get a job since the money that I made during the military Shawn used on bills and fixing up the house. I had a step-daughter and a baby due anytime. Then on top of all of that, even though Shawn and I had been married for over a year, this was the first we had lived together as a married couple. So we had a lot to get used to in addition to me learning to be a civilian again.

Being in the Navy, I was used to being deployed for 6 months or longer at a time. With being away from Shawn for extended periods of time, I turned to porn during my deployments to—shall we say—take care of my needs. When I returned home, as much as I missed Shawn, I had gotten use to porn. I knew exactly what I liked and what would work for me. Shawn wanted to make up for missed time in the first 3 days of returning home. She had even bought a book with different ideas for spicing up our sex life. I just wasn't used to that.

And women always want more than just sex. That was something else I wasn't used to. With porn, I didn't have to worry about taking care of someone else. I just took care of me, and it was done. I was new to being a dad and a husband. I was a proud father, but once we returned home from the hospital, I had to go to work and support the family.

I was just returning home and trying to unwind and get used to life outside of the military. I had lived out of a bag for 4 years, and it was all my belongings that I carried everywhere with me. But not only that, it was a huge chunk of my life right there in those bags. It was a lot of memories that I needed time to deal with and process. It was just a lot hitting me all at once, and I needed time to adjust; time that Shawn wasn't giving me.

Shawn

Justin started having nightmares shortly after our daughter was born. He would start yelling in his sleep and kicking and hitting things. I made the mistake one night of grabbing his arm trying to wake him up.

He raised his head up and pointed to his arm and said, "You see this? I will kill you with it."

That completely freaked me out! I could barely sleep the rest of the night. The next morning I was so scared that I did everything I could to avoid Justin. Well, it didn't take him long to wonder what was going on. I told him that he scared me to death and told him what he had done. He didn't have a clue what I was talking about. I couldn't believe that he didn't remember telling me that he would kill me with his arm, but by the look on his face I could see he was telling the truth.

Over the next few months, the nightmares continued. I quickly learned that it was dangerous to be in the bed with Justin when I tried to wake him up from one of them, so I developed a way of waking him up that kept me safe. I would stand at the door of the bedroom and use a broom to lightly prod his feet with the handle while saying his name, softly at first, then louder. If he woke up especially violent, I could easily duck out the door until he calmed down. Sometimes we also used a bundle of pillows between us to keep him from elbowing me in his sleep. It was yet one more way his attitude was coming between us, this time literally!

We also fought a lot, and I started to notice some other things that Justin was doing.

For starters, Justin would not answer the phone. He would go to great lengths to not have to say hello. It did not matter what I was doing, he would run with the phone and give it to me to answer. It drove me nuts. I could be in the shower, and if the phone would ring, here would come Justin, running across the house, and as soon as he got in the bathroom, he would push the talk button and shove the phone in the shower with me.

Something else came up one night while we were watching a movie. I casually asked him what he would do if we were in a hostage situation like in the movie. Don't ask me what made me ask that, but I did.

He looked at me and, with no emotion whatsoever, said, "I'd shoot you."

I started in on him with, "I'm your wife, and you would shoot me? Without hesitation, you would just shoot me?"

Justin looked at me like I was crazy and said, "Yes, I would shoot you if you were in between the person with the gun and my shot."

I tried to get him to understand that his answer was not a normal one. If the roles were reversed I could not and would not shoot him. "When you love someone, you do everything you can to protect them from harm, not put their life in jeopardy by shooting them."

I could feel the lump forming in my throat. I blinked my eyes to fight back the tears. I sat there for a moment hoping he would say something, *anything*. But Justin just sat there staring at me. It was like he had this 1,000 yard stare and no one was upstairs.

I slowly closed my eyes and swallowed, trying not to get choked up. I looked back up at Justin and said "But you would try to get me away first, right? You would do something right?"

And then I smiled slightly because I knew in my heart that he was going to say yes.

"No," he replied.

My mouth dropped, and I got butterflies in my stomach. *Who was this heartless man?* But once again I thought, *He will be okay. He is just having a hard time adjusting to being home. It will be all right soon.*

Justin was also starting to become very reckless behind the wheel. One time he was angry and driving like a madman. I was scared to death and told him to let me out of the car. When he refused I started telling him to pull the car over immediately. He started yelling at me and then all of a sudden slammed on the brakes on one of the busiest streets in our city, sending me headfirst into the dashboard. I flung the door open, jumped out of the car as fast as I could, and started walking. About five minutes later, he came to me apologizing and begging me to get back in the car.

Fortunately for me, he never pulled that stunt again, but the road rage didn't get any better. If he was in a car and got mad, you had better believe it was the pedal to the metal as he was screaming at the vehicle he felt was in the wrong.

Justin

On top of trying to adjust to being home, my nightmares started. But to be real honest, I couldn't tell you much about them. I don't really remember them, nor do I remember ever attacking Shawn in my sleep. But with as freaked out as she was by the whole thing and her account of what I was saying, I knew it had to be true. I just really didn't think that it was anything to be concerned over. They were just nightmares from things I saw and experienced while in the Navy. I figured that they would go away fairly quickly.

Shawn made a big deal over me not wanting to answer the phone. I just didn't want to talk to anyone, and if it was anything about bills, Shawn was the one that handled things so why would I need to worry about answering the phone. I guess I didn't see that avoiding answering the phone was such an issue with her.

Then came the night we were watching the movie together. Yes, I told Shawn I would shoot her. Maybe my response was crude and mean, but *damn it*, that was what I was taught to do. Any emotion and empathy was trained right out of me. She asked the question, and I gave her the truth. In the military, you don't fight with kid gloves on. And you sure as hell don't worry about someone's feelings. You tell it to 'em straight how it is.

I also was very sure of my training. I knew, even if she realized or not, that I could shoot her without killing her. I thought she would see it as I was saving her, but obviously she did not. I didn't understand why she was so upset. I mean it wasn't like that would ever really happen. Why do women always have to make things so complicated?

As far as the road rage, I didn't realize how bad it was getting. I can't stand stupid people that aren't paying attention, and I can't stand feeling trapped. When I go into a rage it is like I just snap and have no control over it. It's one of those things I just can't explain.

I thought things would get better if I went back to doing what I loved doing best, so I applied for a job as a police officer. But when I took the test at the end of September, I failed. I would have to wait a year and a half before applying again.

SHACKLES

September 2004 — May 2005

In the fall of 2004, Justin had to work two part-time jobs to make ends meet. He never thought it would be so difficult to find a job coming out of the military. Justin worked second and third shift, and I worked first, so that didn't leave us much time to see each other. With Justin's schedule, our daughter had to go to daycare while I was at work, and that meant I had all the responsibility of taking care of the baby while he worked.

You would think that with us not seeing each other, things wouldn't be too bad. But it seemed what little time we had together we spent fighting. The smallest things would send Justin into a rage. He yelled if the baby cried and he had to get up, if he forgot where he put something and couldn't find it, or I didn't do things the way his family had taught him to do. And it took nothing to set him off. It could be anything from someone looking at him to our neighbor stepping in our yard. He would get upset over other people that had nothing to do with us. One minute he would be fine, the next he was angry and screaming.

One time when he was upset about something, I went to a friend's house and stayed two nights. I was determined to teach him a lesson. I wasn't going to call or come home unless he contacted me. He never called or came looking for me. I started questioning then if Justin really loved me or not. When he was home he would sleep, sit and watch TV by himself, or say he was running somewhere and be gone for hours.

It was at this point that I discovered he had a problem with pornography. I was completely crushed and angry. I couldn't understand why he would rather watch that than be with me. I mean, he had a warm body right next to him, but he enjoyed watching some girls on the TV that he couldn't even touch. But once again he had an excuse for that. He told me that with being in the Navy for so long, he got used to that because it was against the rules to be with women on the ship. I told him I understood but that he was home now and had a wife who was more than willing to take care of him. I might as well have been talking to a wall.

Things got worse when I found out he was both talking about our issues with women at work and flirting with online girls. I told him that our lack of intimacy and the way he was acting was going to drive one of us into having an affair.

At that point I started recommending counseling, telling him that I thought he was just having a hard time adjusting to being home and to civilian life. Just the way he was acting made me think he was miserable at home and would rather be back on the ship.

Justin

I touched a little bit on porn earlier, but by now months had gone by, and Shawn and I were working totally different schedules. I worked two jobs to make ends meet, and she was on first shift, so that didn't leave much time for us to have a sex life. By the time the baby was born and Shawn took the full 6 weeks to heal after the C-Section I had been home about 3 months. In that time my nightmares were starting to kick in and so was my anger. We didn't know at the time that it was PTSD. I didn't understand what was going on. All I knew was that once Shawn was cleared by the doctor she was ready to go and I wasn't.

I had too much going on to even begin to worry about sex. Plus I was satisfied with porn. I didn't need anything else. I loved Shawn, but felt completely detached from her. When we did have sex it was just a physical act. I was stuck. She cried when I wouldn't have sex with her, but then she would cry when we did and it wasn't what she was looking for. With porn, there were no expectations at all.

After a while, Shawn really started to drive me nuts. It got to where she wouldn't even let me sleep unless I gave in to her demands. I would just doze off when she would start yelling at me again. After an hour or so of this, I would finally give in to her.

But then she would get all bitchy and say, "See? We could have done that an hour ago!"

Then came the night that Shawn found my stash of porn. When I walked in the door and saw the computer sitting there with porn playing, and my stash of DVDs broken and in the trash, I knew this was not going to be good. Of course I turned the argument back against her. I told her she expected too much of me, that she was a sex-crazed maniac, and that maybe if she didn't always yell at me that I might be interested in it. I also told her that her crying every night because I wouldn't give her sex was a major turn off and if she really loved me that she would leave me alone and understand that I just wasn't interested in sex.

It wasn't just one fight; it was many fights over many days. And of course the fact that I was talking to other women came up, but no matter how many times I told her it wasn't an affair she was not budging on that one. To her I had an affair: Not a physical one, but an emotional affair.

I told her, "You run and talk to your girlfriends; how is that any different than me talking to my female friends?" Shawn then informed me that it was *very* different because she wasn't turning to other males. Then she asked me how I would feel if she started talking to other men? I told her I got it. That solved that problem but left so many more that seemed unsolvable. I fully expected Shawn to call it quits at that point. But she didn't.

Shawn

I listened to what Justin said over the course of our fights, and I just wasn't going to accept that he was happier watching porn than actually being with a woman. So I decided to take matters into my own hands. Men are visual, so I started dressing a little more revealing, putting on makeup when he would come home, and became a tease.

I also talked to LeeAnn who told me, "A man wants a lady in the living room, a cook in the kitchen, and a whore in the bedroom." I knew if I wanted to keep my man something would have to change. I would have to give him everything he wanted. It was going to take some work and time, but I had to fix our sex life. If we connected there, somehow the rest of our relationship would work itself out. I was his wife, and his sexual happiness was my responsibility.

Justin

Shawn became very focused on me and what I wanted and needed in the bedroom. Since she had gotten rid of my porn, I had nowhere else to turn but to her. Slowly but surely our sex life was becoming better and better, but we still didn't have that emotional connection that Shawn kept talking about. She kept saying I didn't *lust* for her, but how could I when I didn't even know what lust was?

So I decided one night to sneak back out on the computer and try to get the enjoyment that I had once had by watching porn. As I turned off the computer, out of nowhere Shawn said, "I hope you saved some for me." I was embarrassed but yet more turned on for Shawn than I ever had been. She caught me, and instead of screaming and throwing me out, used it to make things exciting. After that things changed between us in the bedroom and got *a lot* better. To this day, I can't hear the song *Hanky Panky* by Madonna without thinking about that time in our lives and smiling, even though sometimes I might turn a bit red.

Shawn

At that point, I had very few choices. I could let his watching porn eat at me and make me feel insecure or accept it and have fun with it. When I asked Justin if he saved some for me, even though I couldn't see his face, I knew he had the whole deer in the headlight look just because he froze and didn't say a word. I didn't say anything else and let him stew for a few minutes. I watched as he started to walk down the hall to our bedroom with his head hung down. He was so doing the walk of shame, totally expecting me to start screaming and throw him out. When he got to our bed he stood there for a moment looking at me waiting for me to do or say something, but I didn't. I rolled over and turned my back to him. As I felt him try to gently climb into bed, I waited until he laid down to roll over and pin him to the bed. No way was I going to lose my man because he wasn't satisfied with me. For the first time I let go of my expectations and my needs and put him and his needs first. This was the night I had waited so long for, and it was magical. Afterwards I told Justin, "Now *that* was lust!"

Now that I had Justin's *full* attention, I didn't want to lose it. So I made an extra effort to do things for him that I knew he would like. I helped us connect in the bedroom by wearing sexy clothes I knew would turn him on, tried different things like role playing, watched sexy movies like *9 ½ Weeks* together, and most of all kept it fun.

I didn't like him watching porn, but it was something I was willing to live with so long as he would stop talking to other women. I finally had a glimpse of hope that things were going to get better because our problems seemed to be getting under control. I didn't know things were about to get a lot worse.

WAR

May 2005 — February 2007

Shawn

In May of 2005, Justin got a job at Toyota installing AC units in mini-vans on the assembly line, and I remember thinking, *Finally! Maybe he won't be so stressed all the time now.* Well that was wishful thinking. It seemed like even though he had this dream job, things were only getting worse. We fought all the time, mostly because I had to work, get the baby to daycare, pick the baby up at the end of the day, take care of the baby while Justin was at work, and manage all the responsibility of the house too. I cooked, cleaned, paid the bills, did the laundry, yard work, and shopping, and ran whatever errands that needed to be done. I might as well have been a single parent with a roommate that I never saw but had to clean up after every single day.

Then to make matters worse, when we would fight, Justin would pull his family into it. When the house didn't get cleaned, I would hear from his family how Justin worked and I needed to take care of the house. If I woke Justin up because I needed his help or some rest, I would hear how Justin needed his sleep. What about me? To his family, everything was my responsibility. Living with him was like failing a job that ran 24/7.

I could tell the stress was really getting to Justin. His face no longer looked like the teenage face he'd always had in the past. His skin was starting to get lines around his eyes and mouth, and his hair was going grey at the temples. He wasn't even 25 yet!

On top of it all, I felt alone and betrayed. I had no time for friends or even myself. I had no one to talk to or to have any type of conversation with other than the baby. I couldn't tell my friends—not even LeeAnn—what was going on. I knew if I told them how bad things were, they would start to hate Justin.

I was pissed at everyone and everything. I was depressed, lonely, exhausted, overwhelmed, and felt unloved and unappreciated. But I had no one to talk to, so I kept all my emotions bottled up inside. It wasn't long before I started giving Justin the cold shoulder and acting like an outright bitch to everyone.

After many lonely days and nights spent crying all by myself, I decided Justin's job was not for us. Yeah the money was real good, but I wanted my family back. And that became the new theme for our fights. I didn't care about all the money we had. And Justin was always quick to spend it like he had something to prove. It was almost like he was trying to use material things to satisfy himself.

I thought to myself many times, *How did I get in this position? What did I do to deserve being treated like this?*

Justin

In 2005 I finally got a good job. "It's about freaking time!" was all I could say. I had served my country for 4 years, I came home, and had a hell of a time finding a good job. It didn't matter to employers that I was a veteran. But I did finally get the job at Toyota, and it had very good benefits. Shawn's and my relationship up till this point was rough, but we both thought that by me getting this job things would get better. Man was that ever wishful thinking.

I had to be at work at 4:45 p.m. Work was 45 minutes away, so I left the house at 3:30 p.m. every day. Then I worked until 2:45 a.m., so it was 3:30 a.m. before I would get home. By the time I would unwind and go to bed, it was about 5:30 in the morning. Shawn would get up at 6:30 a.m. to get ready for work, get the baby ready, and then take her to daycare so she could be at work by 8:00 a.m. But it was only a few months before Shawn started staying home.

I think Shawn hated that job more than me working two jobs! She was so angry all the time. I couldn't understand it. I had a good job, had insurance, and was making damn good money.

Saying she was an, "outright bitch," is about right. All she did was bitch about what I wasn't doing. And yes, I would talk to my family about it, and they agreed with me. I worked and brought in the money. I shouldn't have to do anything. My job was longer hours and more money, so watching the baby, cooking, and cleaning were her responsibility. I worked long hours and just wanted to relax when I was not at work. I told Shawn many times that we should trade places just so she could see how good she had it.

I was angry all the time and didn't know why. My family and friends said it was because I wasn't happy in my marriage. They also told me not to put up with her crap, that I didn't deserve it. But then Shawn started to come between me and my family by not letting me talk to them. It's like it was her mission to bust up the bond I had with my family by making me choose between her or them.

She also at one point told me I could no longer make decisions, that I had to run everything I did through her. I was humiliated and felt like she was treating me like a child.

All that did was make me want to spend more money. Buying things made me happy. I worked for that money! And when you face death as much as I did in the military, you tend to want to enjoy the here and now. At any moment your life could be over, and I intended on living my life, not saving for a future I may never have.

Shawn

Finally, I'd had enough. During of one of our fights, I told Justin I didn't care about all the nice things we had. I told him I would rather live in a shack if it meant getting my husband back. That obviously didn't sit very well with him.

He flew into a rage calling me ungrateful and every other name you can think of. Normally at this point, I would go off by myself to cry and let him go to avoid a bigger conflict, but for some reason I decided to open my mouth. I told him he was materialistic and that his toys meant more to him than his family. Never in my wildest dreams could I have imagined the events that happened next!

The next thing I knew, he went back to our bedroom, got his gun, and brought it right back into the living room. I took a step back, not sure what he was going to do. I know he saw the horror on my face, but I had pushed him too far. He got right in my face, cocked the gun, and started selecting targets one by one: the TV, the couch, the table... Then he yelled at me, "What do you want me to shoot? I'll take it all out myself. There will be nothing left. I will shoot this whole fucking house up."

I was terrified. With him being 6' tall and me only being 4'9", I felt like he towered over me. I fell back on the couch not sure whether to look him in the eye or not. All the while thinking, *This is it. I'm gonna die.* I let him yell and scream, and I didn't say a word. I didn't know if I might say something that would set him off and make him start shooting.

He stayed in his rage for what seemed like forever, until finally he put the gun down, looked at me, said, "Do what you want," and walked out the door to go work.

I sat there after he left trying to figure out what just happened. I had never seen him so angry. It was like he snapped and had no control over his actions. I really don't know why I didn't leave the house running and screaming. I've never been so scared in my life.

When I finally pulled myself together, I called the VA hospital to try to get him in to see someone. They asked me if he was a disabled veteran.

"What do you mean, like lost a limb or was shot or something? No he's not," I replied.

They told me that he didn't qualify for any veteran's benefits at that time since he wasn't a disabled veteran and that he needed to find a psychiatrist to speak to.

"Are you kidding me?!? He was fine before he got sent to war. Now there is an obvious problem, and he can't get help? He pulled a gun on me, and you won't see him?!?" I screamed.

I was so mad at that point that before I hung up the phone I told them, "You broke him. Now you need to fix him!"

Their reply was, "I hope you can find him help."

So it was either take him to someone that has no clue what he's been through or fix him myself. I decided I had enough love for both of us that I could help him adjust to not being in the military and be happy again.

But making Justin change wouldn't be an easy task. I decided the change had to start with me. If he was getting angry and yelling, I would agree with him. If he wanted to do something, we did it. I did anything to make Justin happy. At that point I felt that walking on eggshells was the best way to handle the situation. I started watching for people or circumstances that might "set him off." I tried to make sure everything stayed in line, that nothing aggravated or upset him. I had to make sure that everything was "perfect" for him to try to stop the angry outbursts.

I also started a journal at that point. It was a good release for my emotions, being that I had no one I could turn to. Every day, I would sit down and write about things that had happened and how I was feeling. I wasn't very good at it at first, but then I learned a trick to writing. With a computer program that I bought, I no longer had to write. I could put on some headphones with a microphone and start speaking. I no longer worried about spelling, grammar, or if sentences flowed together. I would just say it like I was talking to someone else, and it would write everything I said into my word processor. With no one else to talk to, my computer became the only one who listened to me.

Justin

One night Shawn decided she was going to take everything that I had worked for away from me. She wanted me to quit my job and us to sell everything and live in a shack. Yeah, by this time I had decided she was completely crazy. But she didn't stop there. The whole time she kept talking, I was getting more and more angry. She was threating my life, everything I worked so hard for.

I went into a rage; that's the only way I can explain it. It's like this feeling of being so mad and not being able to control it, kind of like David Banner when he turns into the Incredible Hulk. I just wanted her to shut up and thought, *I'll be damned if she's going to take everything away from me!*

I immediately starting thinking about my training: *Women can no longer be trusted. Everyone is the enemy.* So I went to get my gun to protect my life.

With the gun in my hand I actually felt like I was in control again. When I came out and cocked the gun in her face, I knew what I was doing. I wasn't going to shoot her; I had been trained for this: Scare her until she gave me the information or action that I wanted. And that is exactly what I did. I saw nothing wrong with it because that is what I was trained to do in the military. And at no point through the course of this did I ever view it as abuse.

I had no idea that Shawn had called the VA. She never told me. I honestly doubt at that point I would have gone to a counselor, though. I didn't think I had a problem. It was her; she was the crazy one.

But things with Shawn did start getting a little bit better after that. She stopped yelling at me all the time, we didn't fight near as much, and our sex life was great. Shawn became the wife every man would love to have. She took care of the kids, let me sleep, cleaned the house, cooked the meals, did the laundry, and got on my schedule. And when I came home from work, she would always have a nice surprise for me that had something to do with sex. Things were so great that I didn't need the porn any longer. She wasn't doing much to piss me off, so I didn't see that there was a problem. I thought she finally got it!

Shawn

By August 2005, I was pregnant with our son, and things were feeling like normal, well, as normal as can be for not seeing each other and me really not speaking when we were together. I shouldn't say, "not speaking," but only speaking about what Justin wanted to. Our new normal was me catering to Justin every day and being his slave. I was no longer my own person. I didn't verbalize any complaints or feelings, but my plan was somewhat working. For the most part it kept the peace around the house, and I really felt like we were starting to get back to being a normal family.

But like always, feeling somewhat normal was just a temporary thing. By November things were starting to unravel fast. I passed 70 kidney stones in 7 months, and I spent 7 months in the hospital when I was pregnant with my son. I had surgery after surgery. They placed a tube in my back with a bag to try to keep me from passing more kidney stones, but it wasn't working.

I would go in the hospital, and they would keep me for 3 or 4 days then load me up with morphine, just to send me home for a day or two and do it all over again. The events over those months passed in a drug-induced blur, and I don't really remember much about them. I had around 10 surgeries in those 7 months. They even went in and blew up all the kidney stones thinking that would fix it, only to have me readmitted 4 days later with my kidney full of stones again.

Every time they sent me home and I had pain a few days later, I would have to call Justin home from work to take me to the hospital. His family didn't like that, and all I kept hearing was, "You don't need to bother Justin at work."

Ok, so what exactly am I supposed to do if I don't call Justin? I remember thinking that every time I was told not to call him.

Then of course when I was at home, Justin always wanted sex. *Are you kidding me?* That was the last thing I wanted or needed! I felt like I didn't even have time enough for myself, much less anyone else. Being pregnant had turned my hair a darker shade than it usually was, and I didn't even have the energy to dye it back to blonde. I had lost all my sex drive, I had a tube coming out of my back with a bag attached to it that collected my urine, and my pregnant belly looked like I was smuggling a basketball. Hell no, I didn't want to have sex! And I had no problem telling him I wasn't interested in it.

My girls were being bounced from place to place, never knowing where they would go the next night. And all the while Justin was living a carefree life. He went to work, came up to the hospital after to get some sleep, and woke up an hour before he had to go back to work. I was a basket case missing my girls, but not seeing them for long periods of time didn't seem to bother Justin in the slightest bit. I knew deep down in my heart that he must still love us all, or why would he stay? But he wasn't doing much of anything to show us how much he cared. Lying in the hospital one night, I came to the realization that my husband wasn't passionately in love with me. He also cared about our children only as much as he *could*, which wasn't as much as I thought he *should*. I had to decide if I wanted to leave or continue living like this.

Looking back over the past two years, there wasn't much reason to stay. But then I thought about our two beautiful kids, our first house, the man I fell in love with, and our marriage vows that I held sacred in my heart. *In sickness and in health.* How could I walk away? This was my husband, and whether he knew it or not he needed me.

So after my son, Jaxson, was born, I decided to be a stay-at-home mom. I figured that way I would be able to see Justin a little bit more, the kids would be able to see their dad, and I would be able to fix Justin's issues. Staying at home was a big adjustment for me, not to mention having a newborn and trying to get Jesse adjusted to being back home and having a baby brother. The first few weeks I don't think I got more than two hours of sleep a night because my son had colic.

And then one night I found out my son would sleep with a vacuum cleaner running. Finally, I was getting some sleep until Justin walked in the door to all the lights in the house on and the vacuum cleaner running. As soon as he turned it off, my eyes shot open, and my son started screaming. I jumped up and quickly turned the vacuum cleaner back on. The sound must have startled Justin because he turned around and ripped the cord out of the wall. He started yelling about how this stuff can't happen. I was in no mood to argue so I just said, "Okay."

Justin

Okay, so Shawn gets pregnant, and all of a sudden our life gets crazy. She was always sick; I mean anything she ate made her sick. At 3 months, she was passing kidney stones and living in the hospital.

I worked nights, so there was no daycare I could put Jesse in, and then during the day I would have to get my sleep. Plus I was sleeping at the hospital, so I never really got good sleep. I missed Jesse, but having her wasn't an option. I would have her on the weekends when I wasn't working, though.

As far as the sex thing went, yes I wanted to have sex. I missed everything with Jesse's pregnancy, but I was there for all of Jaxson's. Shawn turned me on, and being pregnant made her glow like I had never seen. Her kidney tubes coming from her back didn't bother me, and I tried to get her to understand that and be comfortable with me. I was having a very hard time going from a great sex life to nothing. I just wanted to be with my wife.

One night, after Jax was born, I walked into the house at almost 4 o'clock in the morning to all the lights on and a vacuum cleaner running while Shawn was passed out on the couch. I didn't know what was going on. So yes, I unplugged the vacuum cleaner. When Jax started crying, I just assumed it was his feeding time, so I continued down the hall to turn off all the lights. When Shawn plugged the vacuum cleaner back in, it scared me to death. Then she gave me a dirty look and went to lie back down on the couch without saying a word. *Why didn't she explain what was going on?* So I was clueless. I told her it was burning electricity as well as ruining our vacuum cleaner by leaving it on and setting it in one spot, and there was no way I could get any sleep with that thing going. She just said, "Okay," and started rocking Jax. I can't help what I don't know.

Shawn

I really felt at this point that so long as I continued to walk on eggshells and put up with Justin's rants that things would get better and would continue getting better. But this was where it got dangerously worse.

A month after our son was born, Jesse was so freaked out by a storm that she kicked a candle off the table in a rage, and that started a fire. We didn't lose the house, but we lost a lot of our belongings. Plus the place needed to be cleaned from all the heat, smoke, and water damage. The thing I lost that meant the most to me was that letter from Justin that he had sent me when we were first dating. First I had lost the sweet guy who had written that letter, and now I had lost all evidence he ever existed.

Justin took a few days off work to help me with everything that needed to be done with the insurance company and then returned to work the following Monday. For two weeks we lived in a hotel, and it was a nightmare with the two kids. During the week Justin worked, and then on weekends we were supposed to get some stuff done rebuilding the house. But that didn't work out the way we thought it would.

Justin got his step-dad involved since he had a buddy who worked for a home remodeling company. All of a sudden he was calling the shots. Justin wanted to help, and the kids being around during the fire clean up on weekends made things difficult. So he expected me to keep the kids at the hotel by myself while he worked at the house. No way was that going to happen!

But then one-day Justin pulled one of his disappearing acts and left me stuck in the hotel with the kids for hours. I called his phone every five minutes, and he kept telling me he was finishing up at a friend's house and would be home shortly. He didn't realize I knew he was lying. I knew he was working at the house because that is what his step-dad told him to do. He even tried to tell me it was taking so long because he got pulled over. When he got back, I was mad, and for the first time since the incident with the gun I spoke my mind.

I told him I knew he was lying, I knew where he was, and that I knew he didn't get pulled over because I called the police dispatch and they had no record of him being pulled over. Okay, so I was bluffing, but Justin didn't know that. Justin started yelling in a rage again, so I told him to get out. When he told me no, I grabbed him by the shirt and tried to force him out the door. He turned around, grabbed me, and slammed me back into the couch. It was the first time he ever put his hands on me in a rage.

Once things calmed down and we talked, we actually got a lot accomplished. I told him I couldn't take someone telling us what and how to do things. We were adults and more than capable of doing things ourselves. If they wanted to help, that was fine, but I *would not* let them run our lives.

I explained to him that if I had the kids all the time I couldn't find us an apartment we could live in until the house was fixed. I needed to be at the house to help clean it out and make a list of things that needed to be replaced, and I needed time to shop and get prices for the insurance company so we could start replacing everything. So Justin agreed that we needed to put the kids into daycare while all of this was going on.

The problems with my kidneys dragged on for months and months. I was in and out of the hospital all the time, which just added to the circus of our lives. Justin decided to use his family medical leave to help me at nights with the kids, get me to my doctor appointments, and help me with everything that needed to be done on the house.

As nice as him using his family medical leave to help us sounded, it didn't quite work out as planned. Justin wound up spending a lot of his time playing video games. He would get so caught up playing war games and racing games that he would completely ignore the house and the kids and wouldn't come to bed until 4 or 5 in the morning, and then he couldn't get up the next day. But the worst were the nights I needed to go to the hospital because I was in so much pain. Justin refused to take me, or he told me just to take some pain pills and wait it out. *Are you kidding me?!?* Believe me, I had passed so many stones that I knew if I needed to go to the hospital or not. I just couldn't get him to understand that the painkillers at home didn't work as fast or as well as the ones they put in an IV at the hospital.

One night, he actually took me to the hospital and dropped me off. He was supposed to come get me when I was finished. I called and called and *called* for over an hour. Never once did he answer, so I had to walk home from the hospital after receiving heavy pain killers through my IV.

It was things like that that made me think Justin didn't give two hoots about me. I wouldn't expect him to drive himself to the hospital if he was doubled over screaming in pain. But with Justin it was all about him. He wasn't going to go out of his way to help me unless it was something he wanted to do. He either didn't give a shit about me, or he only cared about himself. At this point, I just wanted my house back and Justin back to work.

Justin

I don't know what she expected from me during this time. We put the kids in daycare, I took off work to help her out since she was sick, and I helped with everything from the house fire. Hell, I even put up with Shawn and her mother picking everything out for the house. Don't get me wrong, Shawn's mom was a huge help, but when I picked something out that I wanted, Shawn and her mom made the decisions that always ended up being what I didn't want. Shawn even gave her parents the first few insurance checks. So if we wanted something that her mom felt was too expensive or not a necessity, she would only give us what she thought we needed along with a big lecture about how fast we were blowing through the money. I felt like I had no say on anything. *Hello! I am the man of the house here!*

So when the big insurance checks for the contents came, I kept them. That pissed off Shawn's mom, so she refused to help any longer. Hey, that's fine. She helped Shawn pick out all the colors in the house, and we had already replaced the big furniture so that was all done. All that had to be done was finishing the work on the house and moving us back in, which would take a month or two. But I continued to stay at home on medical leave to help Shawn out.

I took her to all her doctor appointments, and when she had to go to the hospital, it was easier to stay at home than take two small children to the hospital for hours. It was like she couldn't understand that. And that one time I left her there, it's because it was 3 a.m. when she called, and I had fallen asleep.

I also couldn't understand why she needed to go to the hospital when she had painkillers at home. They weren't going to do anything other than put an IV in and give her painkillers then send her home. There was just no point to have to keep going to the hospital.

Shawn

Once the work on the house was done and we moved back home, Justin returned to work. I was relieved that I would actually get some time every day when I wouldn't have to worry about upsetting him. I finally felt our life was getting into some of a routine at the house. I cooked, cleaned, did all the laundry, and catered to Justin's every need, and things seemed to be going great. I even had the kids down by 8 o'clock every night without a problem since I had been very firm about putting them to bed on their own from the time they were born. I would take them to their rooms, lay them down, kiss them goodnight, and walk out.

But that relief quickly went away when Jesse started acting as violent as Justin did. She was destructive, would go into a rage when I didn't give her my undivided attention, and was physically violent. We found out she had something called Sensory Integration Disorder, which meant she had a hard time feeling anything. She was rough with everyone and everything because she didn't feel any pain herself and had no clue that others did. She also had no idea how hard she was hitting and gripping because her body didn't let her know. Hitting me was an everyday thing for her, and spanking her had zero effect. So Justin's idea was to use scare tactics on her.

He knew she was scared of this Robosapien robot he had, so he would put her in her room, set it outside her door, and laugh while she screamed. I just couldn't do that to her, so I had no way of disciplining her.

I also didn't agree with Justin's way of handling Jesse. One of the times I tried to stop him from being so hard on her, he flew into a rage and threw me across the kitchen. I grabbed the phone and called 911. Before the call went through, he ripped the phone cord out of the wall, but neither of us realized it was a different phone line. The whole time he was screaming and kicking things, 911 was on the phone. I was begging him to just leave and telling him how bad he was scaring me and the kids, but he just kept coming at me until he had me backed up against the wall.

He punched a hole in the wall, barely missing the side of my face. He kept screaming at me and did it again. By this time I was crying hysterically and scared out of my mind. Then he just turned around and left.

I picked up the phone and must hit the off button because within seconds 911 was calling our house. They asked if everything was okay and told me an officer was on his way. I hung up the phone, called Justin, and told him to stay away because the police were on the phone and heard everything.

When the officer arrived, I let him come in and told him everything was fine; we just got in a fight. A few minutes later, a second officer showed up. Again they asked me what had happened, and again I told them that it was just a fight. I said that after Justin had left I was so upset that I had kicked the stuff over and punched holes in the wall myself. Why I protected him I still don't really know. But Justin was so afraid that I was going to send him to jail that it scared him straight. Even though he still yelled at me, that was the last time he ever touched me.

Justin

Shawn was too soft on Jesse; she wasn't a strong parent. That was my thinking as to why Jesse was pulling this crap. She didn't do it with me because she knew what would happen. Putting a little fear in kids doesn't hurt. My dad used to do it to me when I was little. They learn to respect authority and the rules. Same way in the military while I was an MP—we ruled that boat with an iron fist. No one wanted to cross us or for us to come to get them, because they were afraid of what would happen. Fear kept them from doing things they were not supposed to do, and that is how we maintained order on our ship.

Shawn needed to follow suit and run our house like I did. I ran our house just like I ran the ship. I always stayed in control, and it always worked without fail.

I didn't hit her, but she had pushed me too far again. She had set off my rage when I started punching the wall next to her face. I wasn't going to hit her, just scare her again. When she picked up the phone to call 911, she was crazy if she thought I was going to let that call go through. I had to maintain control of the situation.

My anger was not something that was new at this point, it had been getting worse since coming home, but I really felt like it was everyone else. I didn't have the problem; they did. Before getting married, I had never had a problem with anger, so I assumed that Shawn was the problem not me.

But when Shawn called to tell me 911 was on the phone the whole time and that they were on their way out to the house, I was actually scared. She could turn this whole thing into a spousal abuse, and I could go to jail, not to mention this would ruin my chances of ever becoming a police officer. When she didn't do what I expected her to do, I was very relieved. But it scared me enough to realize at any moment she could take everything away from me. I mean when a woman screams abuse, that's it, game over. Even though I never touched her, all she had to do was say that I did, so I decided maybe the physical scare tactics on Shawn weren't such a good idea.

FALLOUT

February 2007 — January 2009

Shawn

That night after the accidental 911 call, we headed down to Justin's dad and step-mom's house. I told Paula what had happened, and we spent the rest of the weekend talking about things. Up until this point, Paula didn't know me very well, but that weekend she got her eyes opened very wide.

Little Jax had an ear infection and stayed up all night screaming. Justin never once got up to help me. The next day I said something about lying down for a little bit, and he asked me, "Well who will watch the kids then?" Paula told me then, "I don't know how you do it with no help at all." I just shrugged my shoulders and went back to the kids without going to lie down.

On the following Monday, I called the VA clinic again asking for help. Once again I was told there was nothing they could do. I was lost and scared to death of what my family's future would hold.

With Jesse and Justin's behavior, I had my hands full 24 hours a day, 7 days a week. Feeling completely hopeless, I sank into a deep depression.

Fortunately, Paula was starting to come around, and we talked on the phone every day. It didn't take her long to understand why Justin always said I was a bitch. Justin would come home from work at 3:00 a.m., then stay up till 7:00 or 8:00 a.m. when it was time for the kids to wake up, and then sleep until an hour before he would have to leave for work. I had the kids 24/7. Justin didn't help with anything, and he spent every bit of money we had. We were fighting all the time, but up until then I had had no one else who understood my side. Finally someone else was able to see what I was going through!

When Justin wasn't around, Jesse would hit me every chance she got. I know you're probably thinking, "It's a two year old. How bad could it be?" Well, it got so bad that I was afraid to go to sleep at night for fear of what she would do.

Between waking up at night with Justin trying to choke me while having nightmares, the fact that the loaded gun was right under Justin's pillow while he was asleep, and the fear of being attacked by my two year old daughter, I was scared to death. How was I supposed to sleep at all?

At one point Paula had seen Jesse smack me across the face and was stunned. It was funny to hear her re-tell the story of what happened to people. She would always say, "The first time I saw Jesse slap Shawn across the face, Shawn wore her butt out. And then Jesse laughed and smacked Shawn again. And then I thought, *This family doesn't need help; they need an intervention!*"

One night Jesse picked up a fork and tried to stab me with it in the back while I was changing the baby's diaper because I wasn't paying attention to her. And then her hitting me in the face became an everyday thing. It didn't matter what I did, I couldn't regain control.

So now not only did I have my husband to deal with, I had an out-of-control toddler. And to make it worse, when she acted out, it would set Justin off. This quickly became a dangerous vicious cycle.

I had a chance to go out of town with LeeAnn to go to a concert. I didn't want to go because I was afraid to leave the kids all weekend with Justin. Paula told me to send Justin, Jesse, and Jaxson camping with them so I could go and enjoy myself. So that is what I did.

By Sunday I was getting phone calls from Paula telling me how mad at Justin she was. He had let Jesse wander off because he wasn't paying attention. Then Jax ran out of formula, and instead of going and getting some, he just gave him regular milk. Paula told me, "I always thought out of all my boys Justin would be the best dad. Boy was I ever wrong on that one!"

Things were so bad that our extended family members were starting to notice. My mother tried to talk to me about how Justin was acting. She said she had never seen me cower like that before. She asked me what she could do because I was being abused. I blew her off and told her I was not being abused. I mean, it wasn't like he was hitting me. I told her that I was not cowering; I just didn't want to start a scene in front of people.

Justin's dad and step-mom also tried to help. Paula talked to Justin about yelling all the time and convinced him to go to the doctor. She set him up with a family doctor who diagnosed him with anxiety and put him on Lexapro. The medicine seemed to help Justin from flying into a rage, but that was about it. They took Jesse and tried to work with her for a bit, then took Jaxson for a while so I could spend one-on-one time with Jesse. As long as it was just me and Jesse, she did pretty well. But the minute anyone else came around, she would turn back into an evil child, and Justin could not deal with the way she acted.

When I thought things couldn't get any worse, in the spring of 2007 Justin lost his job at Toyota. Now I had Justin and Jesse back together 24 hours a day, which only made things worse. Plus, when Justin lost his job he no longer had insurance to pay for his medication, which was the only thing that kept his temper somewhat under control. Now it seemed like anything I said would set Justin off, which would make Jesse destructive and even more physically aggressive.

We were constantly fighting. Justin couldn't find a job, so I offered to go back to work. I worked two jobs for 2 weeks to keep money coming in, and Justin stayed home with the kids. He had always said we could trade jobs anytime so I could see how good I had it. So during that two weeks, I didn't do a thing around the house or help with the kids when I got home from working 15 hours a day.

At the end of that two weeks, Justin was more than willing to go back to work. He decided that I wasn't bullshitting when I said how hard it was to be a stay-at-home parent. Problem was, when I came back home, Justin had not done anything on the house, and the kids' routines and schedules were all messed up. They would no longer go to bed on their own. Now they had to sleep with us and did not like to go to bed. And the house was such a mess that I had to get Justin's step-mom up to help me get it back in order. It took us two full days to get my house clean again!

I figured that would have taught Justin his lesson and that he would start helping me around the house. But no... It didn't take him long to forget how hard it was. For the next seven months, as he worked this job and that, I was expected to do everything again. This was not flying with me. He wasn't holding steady jobs, but he was still spending money like it grew on trees and didn't help me around the house at all. Justin would buy himself anything he wanted, yet I got the third degree when I bought myself a $20.00 fishing pole. So I started giving him hell every chance I got.

It didn't help that I felt like I had to hide everything that was happening inside our house from nosy outsiders. I knew that Justin wasn't abusing me or the kids, but I knew others thought he was. My mom had already said as much, and I knew others would be next in line. I just wished Justin would get a steady job so he wouldn't be around us as much because when he was working steady, there were fewer problems at home.

Things got worse when one of the neighbors called Child Protective Services on us because Jesse got out in the street while Justin was putting the lawn mower up. I knew it was just one of those things that happens sometimes when you turn your back for 10 seconds, but the neighbors seemed to have it out for us because they kept calling CPS over and over trying to say what bad parents we were. They even called when I let Jesse run through the sprinkler in her underwear at age 3 because they didn't feel that was appropriate. Over the next few months, we had like five or six visits from CPS, and every time they told us how clean our house was and in what good condition the kids were. But the fact that they kept coming tapped into Justin's paranoia and made him even more on edge. He kept getting angrier and angrier, and I just wanted it all to stop. Even though I knew Justin wasn't abusing us, I did know he was yelling a lot of the time and doing other things that would be misinterpreted. And I knew for a fact that CPS wouldn't understand or care that it was brought on because of what happened to Justin in the military. As polite as they were on their visits and as good as we did each time, I knew they weren't there to help us at all but to take away the kids if they thought there was a problem. Finally, CPS told us that they were going to start screening the calls to make sure they were legitimate because it seemed to be a pissed off neighbor situation and not anything like abuse. That helped take off some of the pressure, but Justin still was angry a lot of the time.

Our fighting was worse than it had ever been, and I would tell him to get out at least 3 nights a week. I honestly could not take much more. I asked him in the middle of a fight why he married me. I was a single parent, had my own place, and wasn't dependent on anyone. I wanted to know if he hated me so much, why did he marry me and then beat me down till I was nothing?

Justin

When I lost my job things were hard. Tried staying home; that didn't work. The kids were awful and didn't listen. But then I worked, and she started bitching again. I'm the man of the house. I make the money. No way am I going to stand there and get yelled at. This crazy bitch had lost her mind! If she was so miserable, she could have left, but that would have been the way wrong move. Everything was in my name, and she would have gotten nothing out of me, not even custody of the kids. No judge would give them to her when I said how crazy she'd been acting. She couldn't make it without me.

Sometimes she would get so bad that I would go outside and sit in the truck without even running the heater in the middle of winter. I wanted to show her that she made my life so hellish that even freezing sounded better.

If other people were around, I got the chance to shut her up by yelling at her and telling her how crazy she was acting. Shawn would shut up then because she didn't want to cause a scene. It was about my only way of controlling her. The rest of the time, I was miserable.

Why couldn't Shawn see I couldn't handle things anymore? I couldn't hold down a job, the kids were awful, and yet Shawn just kept coming at me. She was yelling at me for everything. She would yell about what I was doing, what I wasn't doing, spending money, not helping her... But when I did help with the kids, I was "too rough" when I was disciplining them. *What the fuck?!?* Everything pissed me off.

Shawn

In April 2008, Justin finally got a steady job. He was having a hard time dealing with the kids, and I figured him having a job would help. But I would be wrong on that, too. He started having a lot of problems with his co-workers, and as the months went on, he started bringing his stress home. His rages started turning towards the kids, and I started questioning him punishing them when he was so mad. And to make things worse, I was starting to notice bruises on Jaxson. Justin's step-mom questioned the bruises, and I assured her that I would remove the kids if I thought they were caused by Justin.

The last straw came in January 2009 when Justin stepped on a toy one night and completely snapped. He started yelling and slamming the toy into the wall until it broke. He turned around and started screaming and cursing at the kids. When Jesse ran in her room, he jerked her up by her arm and started spanking her. I started screaming for him to stop, and he put her down and started yelling at me. I told him to get out of our house or I would call the police. As he stormed out, he knocked Jaxson out of the way. That was too close to abuse for me. They were little people and couldn't protect themselves, so I had to... and I needed help.

COUNSEL

January 2009 — March 2009

Shawn

First thing the next morning, I called Paula and told her what had happened and that I needed her to take the kids for a while. She told me to also bring the gun so it wasn't accessible to Justin. I quickly got the kids and everything together and got them away from Justin for their own safety.

In a last-ditch effort I called the VA and begged them for help. They asked me if he was an OEF/OIF veteran, and I told them yes. They transferred me to a caseworker who talked to me about what was going on. I told her about his rages, the gun, and how he kept going from job to job among many other things. I told her I felt like he couldn't adjust to civilian life and how he was a totally different man since coming home. She asked me if I could get him down there quickly. I told her yes, but I still had questions. I could tell by the way she was talking that this wasn't new to her. It also struck me as odd that for years we could get no assistance from the VA but now we could get help. I asked her about that, and she said that Bush had signed a new law that gave the VA more power to help OEF/OIF returning veterans. So I asked her if a lot of veterans had these problems. Her response was a simple yes.

I was pissed now. When I started trying to ask more questions she said, "I can answer all of your questions when you're here, but I need you to bring your husband down here as soon as possible."

I didn't know how I would get him to agree to go down there and talk to someone, so she told me to tell him that he might be eligible for money compensation if this was due to his time in the service.

I sat there for a few minutes after we got off the phone trying to figure out how to approach Justin. I don't ever remember crying that hard in my life. But I honestly couldn't tell you if it was tears of joy or intense fear. Once I got myself pulled together, I stood up, wiped my face off, and headed straight to the room where my husband was asleep. You would have thought I was 10 foot tall and bulletproof the way I was walking. But I was determined. I knew no matter what, I had to hold my ground.

When I got to the door I stopped, took a deep breath, and then walked in. I had to yell a few times to get Justin to wake up. I waited until he responded and then very bluntly said, "Get up we're going down to the VA. I don't want to hear any arguments. You either go, or I'm leaving you." He didn't say anything, so I stood there for a second waiting for a response. Nothing. So I repeated myself again.

This time he responded as he got out of bed, telling me that I needed to go to counseling not him. So I listened to his rant while he got in the shower expecting at any moment for him to say, "No I'm not going." But he never did. I don't know if deep down he knew he needed to go.

As we were leaving, he asked about the kids. I wasn't going to open that can of worms alone, so I told him they were at Paula's until we were done.

Justin

I wasn't happy with this at all, but I knew she was serious. I knew that look in her eyes; I saw it the day she called the cops on me. So it was either go or lose my family.

I also wanted to prove to her that I didn't have a problem. *I'll go tell them what Shawn wants me to talk about. I'm man enough to admit what I'm doing. They'll tell her, she's the problem, not me.*

And by going it would shut her up. She would stay so long as I was going for this counseling. Even though I didn't have a problem, I was in no position to argue and not go. So I would play her game for a while to keep my family together.

Shawn

Once at the VA clinic, we had to fill out some paperwork. Then we were taken back to an OEF/OIF case worker. She introduced herself and told us about what she did for veterans returning from war.

She looked at Justin and asked him what he did in the Military and why he thought we were there. Every time he answered, he always started with "I guess." "I guess I have anger issues. I guess I'm having a hard time adjusting to civilian life. I guess I scare her and the kids." Everything was, I guess, I guess, I guess... So I sat there and waited until he was finished.

When he was done, the caseworker looked at me and asked what my concerns were. I had made a list of things so I wouldn't leave anything out.

- Nightmares
- Choking me while asleep
- Saying he would kill me in his sleep
- Sleeping with his gun
- Won't answer phone
- Just wants to be alone
- Always has to be in control
- Up most of night and sleeps most of day
- Puts himself where he can see everything
- Threatening me with the gun
- Uncontrollable anger
- Road rage
- Jumping from job to job
- Gets angry at little things
- Punches holes in things
- Doesn't want to do anything that involved crowds
- Our lack of sex life
- Avoided any military parades
- A drug dealer is the same as a terrorist in his eyes
- He didn't seem capable of loving me or the kids deeply
- His kids bother him

When I was finished, she explained that most of what Justin was experiencing was something that a lot of other soldiers were dealing with when they returned home. Then she handed me a pamphlet for PTSD, or Post Traumatic Stress Disorder. I was confused and had many questions as I read through the pamphlet like: How did he get PTSD since he wasn't in combat? And why was it that I was never told what to watch out for or that this was even a possibility?

She answered everything the best she could and explained to Justin that he needed to go to counseling. But first he would need to talk to someone who would determine the best course of treatment. She also explained that if it was found that all of this was caused by his military career, that he would be compensated with money.

I told her with tears rolling down my face, "I don't give a damn about the money. I just want the man I married back."

She nodded as if to tell me she understood and walked out of the room to find out what would happen next.

After she walked out of the room, Justin rolled his eyes, and I asked what that was about. He shook his head and mumbled, "I don't have that, but whatever."

Within 10 minutes she had us talking to a person who would decide what Justin needed. He took us in a room and asked me first what was going on and why were we here. So once again I explained it all. When I was finished, he looked at Justin and started talking to him. I quickly realized I was clueless about the language they were speaking to one another. It was English, but some sort of military thing.

I interrupted and asked them if they could explain what all they were talking about. The counselor told me that Justin wasn't trained for his MP position. He was trained to turn wrenches, not to carry a weapon. He could tell I didn't understand what he was trying to explain, so he tried a different approach. "When Justin took his test for the Navy, it showed he was a good fit in mechanics. That's why he was trained through boot camp and placed as a machinist. Then he got switched to being an MP and carrying a gun, which is not what he was trained for. So it was hard for him to process all the things that happened in his mind. It's like trying to put a square peg in a round hole."

I asked them why the Navy would move a machinist to be an MP if they knew by the testing that someone wasn't a good fit for that position. His response was, "They do it all the time to fill an open position." I just shook my head in disbelief and he continued on talking to Justin.

I started to talk about something he'd asked Justin, but then the counselor looked at me and asked if I wouldn't mind stepping outside so they could talk. "You know, vet to vet stuff." I agreed and went outside to wait for Justin.

Justin came out about 30 minutes later and told me that he had to start seeing a counselor at something called the Vet Center the next day. I asked him if he was okay with all of this, and his response was, "I don't really have a choice, do I?" Not exactly the answer I was looking for, but at least he understood that he had to go. So I didn't say anything else the rest of the day.

Justin

What the hell could I say? I didn't agree that I had PTSD. I mean how could I? I never saw combat. But after talking to the guy, also a vet, for just a few minutes, I realized maybe I was having some issues that I needed to talk out.

He told me, "You were trained as a machinist. You were taught to turn wrenches. Then you get moved, and a gun is put in your hands when you never were trained to deal with that job. So you need some time to process and deprogram."

The Vet Center counselor they were putting me with was also a veteran so I was okay with going to talk to them. They knew what I was going through and feeling. I just couldn't tell Shawn that. I realized she really did care about me, but she didn't get it. She couldn't understand what was going on with me. She was never in the military.

The next day we met the counselor at the Vet Center. She was an intern, but she was a veteran, too, so I was alright speaking with her. She also knew about guns, which I found really cool.

But I was *not* happy when I found out Shawn had moved the kids down to my dad and stepmom's house. *How could she think I was abusing them?* I may have been rough, but it was to scare them. I would never really hurt them. I knew I didn't cause the bruises on our son, but I had to convince Shawn. The only thing I could do was to tell Shawn to take Jaxson to the doctor and get him checked out.

Shawn

Once we got home from the Vet Center and Justin left for work, I got on the phone with Paula and told her what had happened at the Vet Center, what the plan was moving on, and that I would call her after his next meeting.

So the next day, we went to the Vet Center and met his new counselor. She was very nice and told us up front that she was an intern. She also had served in the military and knew a lot about guns, so they had a common bond right there.

The first session was familiar, as in a lot of tears and telling her the same story that we had told the day before. We also talked about the kids, and I explained to both of them that I had moved them out of the home until I got Justin help and saw improvement. That did not sit very well with Justin. He kept saying he couldn't have left bruises on Jaxson and that he didn't hurt him. The counselor realized we had some serious issues and asked us to come back every day for the rest of the week. We agreed and left for the day.

On day two of counseling, we spent a lot of time talking about our daughter and the way she acted. We told her how she refused to listen, how destructive she was, and how when she was 2 years old, she picked up a fork and tried to stab me in the back with it while I was changing our newborn's diaper. We all laughed as I told the counselor about hearing stories of a parent being abused by their kid. People think the kid just needs some discipline or as some people would say "that kid needs a good ass whooping." But when it's happening to you, it's not so easy.

We discussed a few other things and then talked about our son's bruises again. Once again Justin denied hurting Jaxson in any way or giving him those bruises.

As soon as I got home, I called Paula and told her what was going on. I told her how his story never changed and how he stuck to denying that he'd done anything harmful to our son. She sat there for a second and said, "If Justin isn't hurting him, then something else is wrong that would cause him to bruise like this all over." That really got me thinking.

So on day three of counseling, I told Justin that he had one last chance to tell me if he had hurt our son, because if not then something was wrong with Jaxson and I needed to take him to a doctor. But if I took him to the doctor and they said it was abuse, I could not help him and he would have to move out.

Justin shocked me when he told me to please take Jaxson to the doctor. I wasn't expecting that at all. So we decided the next day I would take our son to the doctor and Justin would go to counseling alone.

I woke up early and started getting ready. I called the doctor at 7:55 in the morning and scheduled my son's appointment for 10:45. I drove 45 minutes to pick up Jaxson from Paula's house, and another 45 minutes back to arrive at the doctor's office at 10:20. I sat in my van for 15 minutes arguing with myself.

I tried to think of other ways to handle this and be more supportive of my husband, but I couldn't think of a single one. So I quickly pulled myself together, got my son, and went in to face whatever was thrown our way.

They called us and took us to a room. When the doctor came in she asked what was going on, and I broke down in tears as I explained to her my concerns. I told her Justin was having some anger issues and that my son was bruising a lot. I told her I honestly didn't know if they came from Justin or maybe from something else. The doctor quickly ruled out abuse and started doing blood work to figure out what might be the cause of his bruises.

I called Justin at the Vet Center to let him and his counselor know it wasn't abuse. I asked him how things were going, and he told me they were talking about guns and how relaxing it was to go shoot them. That bothered me because I had a real problem with Justin and guns, but I had other things to worry about.

Words could not express how bad I felt not trusting my husband and accusing him of child abuse when it turned out not to be the case. Every time I tried to apologize, he would cut me off with a, "no big deal" or "don't worry about it." Which, believe me, made me feel much worse.

It took weeks to complete the tests, which told us that our son had something called Von Willebrand disease. This is a hereditary bleeding disorder that results in easy bruising. It was a relief, and it further confirmed that my husband was not hurting the kids. With that information we moved the kids back into the house and focused on counseling.

The first thing I wanted to address was Justin and his guns in the house. I went to counseling expecting them to agree with me and tell Justin that the guns had to go. But shockingly she sat and talked to me about how relaxing it was for Justin to shoot his gun. *What? Are you kidding me?!?* I'm scared to death of this gun, and she's trying to convince me that he needs this as a stress reliever. I felt furious and betrayed. Every time I saw Justin with a gun, even his hunting gun, I was afraid to talk to him. I was afraid to say anything, and I went into a panic attack.

This went on for two weeks, and then all of a sudden she started talking to Justin about getting an air gun. That way he could still have his stress reliever, and I would feel safe because he couldn't kill me with it. It may hurt like hell, but I wouldn't die if he shot me. I couldn't believe it when Justin agreed. I was sold at that point! These counselors knew what they were doing, and I knew my family was going to be okay. It may not be perfect and we still had a long way to go, but it was the first glimpse of hope I'd had in years.

They also got Justin into the VA behavioral clinic. They started trying a few different medications and found that Wellbutrin worked the best for his anxiety. They also gave him a medication used for allergies to help him sleep. I started seeing positive improvements in Justin pretty quickly when we got the medication figured out.

Justin

I wasn't surprised when Shawn called. I knew I'd done nothing wrong, but blaming her for standing up and protecting our kids first was not even cool. She did what she had to do as a mother until she was able to know the kids were safe. I really found myself respecting her instead of being upset.

I just wanted them to hurry up with the test to figure out what was wrong with my son. Through counseling, I realized how much my actions with the gun scared Shawn.

For years I didn't know how scared she was, I really felt bad for what I'd done to her. So when she was fine with an air gun, I had no problem getting rid of the real gun. I wanted her to feel safe with me, not scared of me. I didn't like the idea of having to go on medicines, but I thought I would try them and see if it will help. If it made Shawn happy and feel somewhat safe, I'd do it for her.

Shawn

We continued with counseling at the Vet Center and went to the VA about once a month. I was a sponge for any and all information in our sessions. The one notebook I always took with me was quickly filling up, not just with what the counselor said, but with things Justin said as well. They teased me and called me Queen of the Note-Takers, but nobody, not even me, knew how valuable those notes would be later on.

At our next visit to the Vet Center, the counselor gave me a book called *Veterans and Families' Guide to Recovering from PTSD* by Stephanie Laite Lanham. She said anyone could get it for free at any Vet Center or VA.

She asked me to read through it and make notes in each section of things I saw Justin doing. She also gave me a copy of the DSM Criteria for PTSD and told me to go through it and see where Justin fit. When I first looked at the criteria, it really meant nothing to me. I remember thinking, *You almost need a PhD to really understand it.*

So I started reading the book and hoped that it would give me some answers and help the criteria make sense. What follows here is the DSM Criteria for PTSD and the responses I wrote on the symptom checklist form. After that is my breakdown, line-by-line, in a form that was easier for me to understand.

309.81 — DSM-IV Criteria for Posttraumatic Stress Disorder

A. The person has been exposed to a traumatic event in which both of the following were present:

(1) The person experienced, witnessed, or was confronted with an event or events that involved actual or threatened death or serious injury, or a threat to the physical integrity of self or others
(2) The person's response involved intense fear, helplessness, or horror. **Note:** In children, this may be expressed instead by disorganized or agitated behavior.

B. The traumatic event is persistently re-experienced in one (or more) of the following ways:

309.81 — DSM-IV Criteria for Posttraumatic Stress Disorder

(1) Recurrent and intrusive distressing recollections of the event, including images, thoughts, or perceptions. **Note:** In young children, repetitive play may occur in which themes or aspects of the trauma are expressed.
(2) Recurrent distressing dreams of the event. **Note:** In children, there may be frightening dreams without recognizable content.
(3) Acting or feeling as if the traumatic event were recurring (includes a sense of reliving the experience, illusions, hallucinations, and dissociative flashback episodes, including those that occur on awakening or when intoxicated). **Note:** In young children, trauma-specific reenactment may occur.
(4) Intense psychological distress at exposure to internal or external cues that symbolize or resemble an aspect of the traumatic event.
(5) Physiological reactivity on exposure to internal or external cues that symbolize or resemble an aspect of the traumatic event.

C. Persistent avoidance of stimuli associated with the trauma and numbing of general responsiveness (not present before the trauma), as indicated by three (or more) of the following:

(1) Efforts to avoid thoughts, feelings, or conversations associated with the trauma
(2) Efforts to avoid activities, places, or people that arouse recollections of the trauma
(3) Inability to recall an important aspect of the trauma
(4) Markedly diminished interest or participation in significant activities

309.81 — DSM-IV Criteria for Posttraumatic Stress Disorder

(5) Feeling of detachment or estrangement from others
(6) Restricted range of affect (e.g., unable to have loving feelings)
(7) Sense of a foreshortened future (e.g., does not expect to have a career, marriage, children, or a normal life span)

D. Persistent symptoms of increased arousal (not present before the trauma), as indicated by two (or more) of the following:

(1) Difficulty falling or staying asleep
(2) Irritability or outbursts of anger
(3) Difficulty concentrating
(4) Hyper vigilance
(5) Exaggerated startle response

E. Duration of the disturbance (symptoms in Criteria B, C, and D) is more than 1 month.

F. The disturbance causes clinically significant distress or impairment in social, occupational, or other important areas of functioning.

Specify if:
Acute: if duration of symptoms is less than 3 mos
Chronic: if duration of symptoms is 3 mos or more

Specify if:
With Delayed Onset: if onset of symptoms is at least 6 months after the stressor.

PTSD SYMPTOM CHECKLIST

Anger - The holes in the walls, snapping at everything. We had anger issues.
Anxiety - Irritability and sleep disturbance. We had Anxiety.
Chronic Pain - None.
Compulsion - Everything had to be a certain way.
Confusion - Combative Behavior, forgetting things. Check.
Crisis - Feel out of Control. With Justin everything is a Crisis.
Delusions - Flashbacks. None when awake, but in his sleep
Denial - I needed help; there was nothing wrong with him.
Dependence - I had to handle everything for Justin. I was the man and woman of the family.
Depression - This one was hard because Justin would say no he is not depressed. But agitation, anxiety, withdrawal, etc. are all symptoms. So I would say yes.
Disordered Eating - When Justin first came home he had a hard time with food. They all seemed to make him sick.
Flashbacks - No only Dreams.
Grief - Justin seemed like he didn't care about anything. He had walls built up. It was hard to tell anything.
Guilt - "Survivor's Guilt" I honestly could not answer that.

PTSD SYMPTOM CHECKLIST

Isolation - Justin didn't want to do anything. He didn't go around friends, didn't want to go around people, and didn't want to do things we used to do.
Loneliness - Justin never could talk to me and said I wouldn't understand. He felt like he had no one.
Low Self-Esteem - Justin always had a cocky attitude. He did not have a problem with this.
Obsessions - His gun was his biggest obsession. Along with trying to structure our family lives to be like his military life.
Hyper vigilance - Justin was always on guard. Life was so serious.
Passive-Aggressive Behavior - Everything turned into an angry discussion. He could not reply without being angry or hostile.
Phobia - I did not think Justin had phobias. But he did avoid anything that had to do with Veterans.
Sexual Trauma - None
Sleep Disorders - Justin would not sleep at night and then crash during the day. And once he did get to sleep he would sleep 12-14 hours.
Substance Abuse - None
Suicidal Thoughts or Ideation - None

After filling all of this paper out, I went back and looked over the criteria for PTSD. It still was somewhat confusing to me, so I made my own worksheet out to help me keep things straight.

A. The person has been exposed to a traumatic event in which both of the following were present:

(1) The person experienced, witnessed, or was confronted with an event or events that involved actual or threatened death or serious injury, or a threat to the physical integrity of self or others

(2) The person's response involved intense fear, helplessness, or horror.

This means:

1. You are somewhere where people's only goals in life are to kill you or blow you up.
2. You see friends killed.
3. You help clean up dead bodies.
4. You have to kill someone.
5. You see horrific accidents.
6. You were injured.
7. You are somewhere that you are always watching out because you are afraid of dying.

B. The traumatic event is persistently re-experienced in one (or more) of the following ways:

(1) Recurrent and intrusive distressing recollections of the event, including images, thoughts, or perceptions.

(2) Recurrent distressing dreams of the event.

(3) Acting or feeling as if the traumatic event were recurring (includes a sense of reliving the

experience, illusions, hallucinations, and dissociative flashback episodes, including those that occur on awakening or when intoxicated.

(4) Intense psychological distress at exposure to internal or external cues that symbolize or resemble an aspect of the traumatic event.

(5) Physiological reactivity on exposure to internal or external cues that symbolize or resemble an aspect of the traumatic event.

This means:

1. Nightmares about the incident.
2. Acting out the incident while asleep.
3. Feeling like you're back there when you aren't. You see a fire, and you flashback to being bombed.
4. Feeling like they are boxed in...Road Rage
5. Feeling like everyone is out to get them.

C. Persistent avoidance of stimuli associated with the trauma and numbing of general responsiveness (not present before the trauma), as indicated by three (or more) of the following:

(1) Efforts to avoid thoughts, feelings, or conversations associated with the trauma

(2) Efforts to avoid activities, places, or people that arouse recollections of the trauma

(3) Inability to recall an important aspect of the trauma

(4) Markedly diminished interest or participation in significant activities

(5) Feeling of detachment or estrangement from others

(6) Restricted range of affect (e.g., unable to have loving feelings)

(7) Sense of a foreshortened future (e.g., does not expect to have a career, marriage, children, or a normal life span)

This means:
1. Won't talk about what happened.
2. Doesn't remember things before, after, or during the event.
3. Doesn't want to go out or do things they used to do; It's like they would rather be somewhere else.
4. Standing there staring at you while you bawl your eyes out.
5. Could care less if you stay or go.
6. Doesn't seem to care about anything.

D. Persistent symptoms of increased arousal (not present before the trauma), as indicated by two (or more) of the following:

(1) Difficulty falling or staying asleep
(2) Irritability or outbursts of anger
(3) Difficulty concentrating
(4) Hyper vigilance
(5) Exaggerated startle response

This means:
1. Has trouble going to sleep.
2. Difficulty staying asleep.
3. Angry at little things that would not have mattered before
4. Stupid civilian people get on your nerves.
5. Forgetting things. You ask him for milk while he is out, and he totally forgets.
6. Always on guard. Getting up to check the doors are locked 10 times before bed.
7. Can't handle crowds. Has to be where he can see everything.
8. Hitting the deck when they hear a loud noise.

By the time we went back to the next counseling session we had plenty to discuss. Out of all of these possible symptoms, Justin had quite a few of them. We talked about "triggers" or, in other words, what sets Justin off. We started trying to decide what compromises would need to be made to avoid triggering him. At first the focus was on getting Justin to open up and not be so angry and defensive.

With Justin's temper, we decided it would be best for me to handle all the discipline and for Justin to not be involved with any of it, just until we got some things worked out and under control. We had to get Jesse to not be afraid of Justin and to get her to stop acting out. So I would handle the discipline, and Justin would work with giving her praise and affection.

We knew that Justin would have to change his behavior, and until that happened he could not assume a parent role which was desperately needed. So we decided that for the time being that we should focus on him and work with Jesse along the way.

Justin

With Jesse I struggled a lot. I loved her, but she got on my last nerve. No matter how hard I tried, I couldn't get past the way she acted. She wouldn't listen to me, she destroyed things, and she was just downright mean.

I agreed to do this hoping it would help. I wanted it to work; I wanted things to change, to get better for us. But at that point, I had no idea what that would even look like. I felt like everything I did was wrong. If I disciplined Jesse, Shawn would get mad. If I let Jesse get away with everything, she stopped seeing me as her dad. I couldn't win.

Deep down, part of me was just done with it all. I felt like I was on the outside of the world looking in. I could see it, but I wasn't a part of it. I just wanted everyone to stop hassling me. They kept talking about PTSD, but I didn't think there was anything wrong with me that leaving me alone wouldn't fix.

S.O.S.

May 2009

Shawn

A few days later, I scheduled a one-on-one session with a therapist to talk about how the new plan for disciplining Jesse wasn't working. I was feeling desperate and really needed some advice on how to save our family from just sinking further and further into the anger and violence that was taking over. She told me to come on in so we could talk.

Once I went to the counseling session, I began to tell her how things weren't getting better but actually much worse. Somehow by Justin not being able to discipline her, Jesse no longer looked at him as a parent but viewed him more like an equal. She tattled on Justin, completely ignored anything he said, and now talked back to him. Also, I guess Jesse acting like that made Justin feel like he was no longer the man of the house. So anytime I asked for help with anything, he was like, "Nope. Can't do anything. Remember?" So I didn't know what to do anymore.

I told her, "I just don't know how much more I can take! It's this crazy cycle that's just getting worse. Jesse does something Justin doesn't like, he tells her to stop, she doesn't listen, he starts yelling, she comes and tells on him which makes him even more angry, he starts screaming and slamming doors, and then she will start hitting walls, stomping around the house, and slamming doors. It's like this every single day!"

The counselor explained to me that it sounded like Jesse was mimicking Justin's behavior. It was something called Secondary PTSD or SPTSD. It wasn't recognized by doctors yet but is something they are seeing more and more of in spouses and children. Trauma has taught veterans that at any moment safety could be destroyed, which makes them jumpy and over-reactive as well as somewhat violent. If extreme enough, the actions and reactions of veterans can traumatize the people around them. Spouses and children of veterans with PTSD will sometimes start to exhibit some of the "common characteristics" of PTSD.

She told me that children who are victims of Secondary PTSD have the same kinds of symptoms, but they show up in different ways than they do for the spouses. Children normally tend to respond to the parents PTSD in one of three ways. First, the child experiences secondary trauma and displays many of the same symptoms as the parent with PTSD. Second, the child takes on parental roles. And the third possible response would be the child who becomes emotionally uninvolved, which leads to problems at school, depression, and relationship problems.

I asked the counselor why it would be that only Jesse would have issues and not my other two kids. She told me that my older daughter wasn't around very much due to the custody arrangement, so she wouldn't be exposed to Justin's behavior as much, and Jaxson was so little that he didn't have the skills to really express what was happening in the same way Jesse did.

I thought about it for a moment, and then I realized what she was saying. To make sure I understood exactly what she meant I asked her, "So let me see if I understand this: With Jesse, it's like she is Justin made over? She grew up with her dad punching holes in walls, yelling and screaming about everything, and pretty much acting like he hated us, so that was all she knew. She *learned* that when things didn't go right, Dad yelled, went into rages, and became physically destructive. So she thought that's what you did to deal with things. Is that what you mean?"

She nodded yes, but I was confused. I told her that I understood that Jesse was mimicking Justin's behavior, but it wasn't like I let her get away with acting that way.

The counselor explained that even though I punished Jesse for acting that way, it was what she was seeing with my actions that made her think it was okay. Jesse knew that if she kept acting out long enough she would get what she wanted out of me. The counselor told me that before I could get Jesse under control, I had to deal with my Secondary PTSD. I immediately looked at her and asked her what she was talking about.

She told me that spouses minimize the actions of the veteran or make excuses for their behavior. When Justin came home, I kept making excuses thinking he was just having a hard time readjusting. As things got worse, I excused a lot of bad behavior by thinking I could fix him on my own. I started walking on eggshells, doing anything and everything I could to make sure Justin stayed happy. Even if he was angry about something and I agreed with him, I had to be the rational one and keep him in check. If I expressed my own anger, it would only feed his and make things worse. Sometimes I had to even defend the people I was mad at to keep him calm. But no matter how hard I tried, I was still getting yelled at and blamed for everything that went wrong. That led to me pulling away from my friends a lot of times *because* of the way Justin acted.

I sat there listening and didn't disagree until she said something about my actions being no different than someone in an emotional abusive relationship. I was quick to tell her that I was not being abused. I felt the same way I did as when my mom had tried to tell me that. She didn't understand what it was like, and now, neither did the counselor.

The counselor took a deep breath and tried talking to me again. She said that Justin was doing and saying a lot of the same things as abusers, even though it was the PTSD making him do it and not really who he was and that because of that, I was doing and saying a lot of the same things abused women do. She told me that acting like an abused woman pretty much did the same things to my daughter as if I actually were one, that my reactions to Justin were teaching Jesse how to be abusive herself.

She continued by telling me "Jesse is learning all of this from watching Justin yell at you and basically get his way then. Justin is just doing what you are allowing him to do to you. He doesn't even realize he has a problem. So the fact that you are angry, depressed, and have no hope doesn't even click that his and Jesse's actions are what are causing you to feel this way. They think it's you. You have to start breaking this cycle you are in. Start small. Do you have any friends or family you talk to or do things with?"

I told her about Justin's step-mom Paula. I explained how she helped me with Jesse and Jaxson, that she was someone who both Justin and I can go to and vent without her taking sides or encouraging either of us to leave. If I couldn't keep up with the house, she would always ask if I needed any help. And the best part was if Paula did help me clean my house, she didn't judge or gripe at all. She just helped me.

I also explained how Paula was working with me on keeping my mouth shut sometimes. She helped me see that if I just let Justin gripe and didn't mouth back, that his anger spew would just blow over most of the time. It wasn't the same as walking on eggshells, though. I wasn't cowering in fear. I was just choosing to stay calm and quiet so he would finish faster. It was a case of picking my battles.

The therapist said that was great, but wanted to know if there was anyone else that I had. I told her about my best friend LeeAnn, but explained that our schedules are what kept us apart. I had talked to LeeAnn about many things, but I couldn't tell her everything. She wouldn't understand and would probably want me to leave Justin, so I don't tell her all of what was going on.

The counselor told me that just getting out and away from everything, even if it was only for ten minutes, would do wonders for me. It would also help me not feel so isolated.

We talked for a while longer about Justin's and my feelings. She told me it was okay to be angry and that everything I was feeling was normal for our situation, especially when I explained to her that I felt like part of the problem with parenting was that I took the kids' side over Justin's a lot of times because I felt he was too mean to them. She asked how I protected the kids when Justin was in a rage. I explained that I had made a "safe-haven" in the closet for the kids. When Justin was angry, I would tell the kids to go there until I came and got them. They had color crayons, snacks, toys, pillows, and blankets there. My thought was that the more I kept them out of Justin's line of sight, the less likely it was he would turn and take it out on them.

I also told her about how I always had some kind of backup plan in case something went terribly wrong. I made sure there was always somewhere I could send the kids if Justin got too angry, even if I couldn't go with them right away. Their safety was first and foremost to me. Fortunately, I hadn't had to use my backup plan except for that one time when I initially got Justin into therapy and I left the kids with Paula. I hoped I wouldn't have to use it again.

The therapist told me she needed to spend some one-on-one time with Justin so he could start to see where his actions were not acceptable. Before I left that day, we decided if Justin was alright with it that she would discuss what happened in his sessions with me in the future so that I could understand him better.

When I left that day, I felt like we at least had some sort of plan to get Justin back on track. I was content to let things take their course at this point.

LIFE-VEST

May 2009 — June 2009

Shawn

In May 2009, our counselor's time as an intern was officially up, but she got to stay on a while longer until they found a replacement for her. With counseling, our family was starting to change. Justin was really starting to open up in our sessions, and I was learning to adapt to living with him having PTSD. But a lot stayed the same. Justin was still jumping from job to job since he had come back home, and I realized the job he was working at that point would probably not last much longer. He had been there a little less than a year, and he was starting to have problems with his boss.

We discussed his problems at counseling, and talked about what Justin really wanted to do. His response was simple: He wanted to become a police officer. He had an interview coming up with the sheriff's department, which is further than he had made it the other four times he had applied for a police job. So we were remaining hopeful that this time it would work out. But in my mind I was already concerned. So I started looking for a way to make some extra money on the side, just in case he didn't get the job as a sheriff or lost his current job.

I told the counselor about my plans and work that was already in place to help keep our family afloat. I'd had no clue what to do until one day in February when Justin fixed his broken Xbox 360. I couldn't believe he did it with no problem at all. We started throwing around the idea of fixing broken Xbox 360 consoles. He looked on eBay and was pretty confident it would be easy to fix the RROD (Red-Ring of Death, a circle of red lights on the system indicating it is broken). So I decided to buy two broken Xbox consoles and see what would happen.

When the broken units arrived at our house, Justin eagerly jumped in and started taking them apart. Three hours later Justin was in a rage because he couldn't get them to work. He had pretty much decided that fixing Xbox 360 consoles wasn't that easy and was too frustrating for him. So I told him to explain the whole process to me: Tell me what the problem was, what he was supposed to do to fix it, and why he didn't think it was working.

So when Justin left for work and I got the kids in bed that night, I jumped on the internet and started to do some research. I watched YouTube videos and bought an Xbox 360 repair guide ebook. By the time Justin came home, I'd figured out that he couldn't fix them because he'd nicked the motherboard when trying to take parts off of it.

So I ordered two more broken Xbox 360 units and decided to try it again.

Through my research, I also found out that the way Justin was planning on fixing these Xbox consoles wasn't the right way to do it. So I ordered a hot air rework station like the one I had seen used in a YouTube video. Once everything arrived we tried to repair the boxes with the new machine. Within 2 hours we had repaired both broken Xbox 360 units and put them up for sale on eBay. When they both sold within 24 hours, we had made $50.00 profit on both boxes. So, the next day I ordered 10 more broken Xbox 360 consoles.

After I told the counselor all of this, I said that it felt good to have a plan in place in case things didn't go well with Justin.

The following Saturday, Justin had his interview with the Sheriff's Department. This was the fourth time he had applied for a police officer position since leaving the Navy. But this was the first time he had passed the test and made it to the interview stage.

I waited at home until he got back to see how it went. He told me that they would send a letter in the next few weeks to let him know. While we waited to find out if he had gotten the job, we continued to go to counseling and work on Xbox consoles.

When the letter arrived Justin walked in the house and threw it at me. He had once again been rejected. He went to work that night and decided to work a half day. The problem was that he didn't ask anyone and just left a note on the boss's desk. The next day when he went to work he got suspended for 3 days. When he called and told me, I was dumbfounded. I could not believe he didn't ask his boss if he could use part of his personal day. So I called our counselor and told her what was going on. She told us to come in the next day.

When we got to counseling, we started with me first. I was upset and couldn't believe that Justin had pulled a stunt like that. But when we talked to him, we realized he didn't think he'd done anything wrong. His reasoning was the boss left all the time without telling anyone. He really didn't understand that when someone is a boss they have more freedom than employees do. He kept saying, "In the service," I threw up my hands at that point and told the counselor, "He doesn't get it!"

Then he started talking about not getting hired on as a police officer and how he was better trained for the position then all of the kids coming out of college. She tried to explain to Justin that, whether he realized it or not, his body language and the way he talked could be the reason he wasn't getting hired. She tried to get him to understand that others could tell he was a time bomb waiting to go off, and as a police officer, that was dangerous.

They started talking about his answers to questions in the interview. Listening to him, I just shook my head because even I could tell by his answers that he didn't get hired because he was too programmed by the military. With Justin, everything was black and white, right or wrong. There was no grey area in his mind.

I started thinking about him having a gun again, and that made me really nervous. So I jumped in and started talking about how it was okay that he didn't get the job and how we had started a home business and that would make up the income that he would have gotten by being a sheriff. And if things kept going well with the business, maybe we could get to a point that he wouldn't have to have a job. I stressed that we weren't to that point yet, but we had a good thing going and needed to concentrate on that so he could stay home. A lot of Justin's stress came from having to go to work and be around people.

For the next month we really focused on the Xbox 360 repair business. I worked with a wholesaler to get our Xbox units cheaper and did some work for him in trade. We got to a point where we were repairing 50 broken Xbox consoles every 10-14 days. The downside to all that work and extra money was that it was taking a toll on us. Justin was still working full time, so I had to watch the kids while Justin was at work. Each box took about an hour to repair. After they were repaired, we would have to play on them for an hour or two to make sure they wouldn't break again. Because of that we weren't getting much sleep and our stress level was starting to go sky high. Add the time it took me to list them on eBay, answer questions, ship them off, and handle any returns or complaints, and it was becoming a nightmare!

Then in June 2009, Justin got laid off from his job. I thought it was okay because now we would be able to run the Xbox repair business better with both of us home.

We also at that time filed for disability for Justin's PTSD. He had been in counseling and seeing the doctor at the VA for 6 months now, and they had no doubt he had PTSD. A disability claim seemed like a sure thing.

Working from home seemed to help Justin more than anything. He didn't have the stress any longer of having to be around other people, and there was no boss for Justin to argue with. The only problem was that as our Xbox 360 repair business grew, it put stress back on Justin. I quickly realized that Justin couldn't handle the high demands our business was putting on us. So I was stuck. Having a job didn't work for Justin and neither did working from home.

Justin

I was really angry about not getting the job at the Sheriff's Department. It was total B.S. that they would rather hire some kid who had a college degree over someone like me with actual police experience. I had the best training in the world! It should have been a no-brainer. It was just another example of how civilians didn't understand how to run things. They would rather be politically correct than have someone on their team who could follow rules and regs 100%. I wouldn't have been someone who cut *anyone* a break. The law is the law!

At least counseling seemed to be going well. It was only there that I found any peace about the job issue. I still didn't like it, but at least I kind of understood why I didn't get hired. I also still didn't think I had PTSD, but the counseling was helping me and Shawn, so it wasn't a bad thing. I still had anger issues, I would act before thinking, and I still spent a lot of money, but I was trying. I was making improvements very slowly, but they were improvements that Shawn was happy with.

I was learning to communicate with Shawn much better now. I realized that because I live in the moment, Shawn was always trying to figure out what the future held for our family. She would hope for the best, but expect the worst and have a plan if and when it did happen. So it did not surprise me when she started looking at starting a home business. Shawn is business smart, so I had no doubt we would succeed at anything she decided to do.

Repairing Xbox units wasn't hard once we started doing it, but the "Red Ring of Death" repair wasn't a guaranteed fix. So we got a lot of returns and re-fixes. It helped that Shawn made a deal with with a warehouse where we could do repairs for them in exchange for broken Xbox consoles. The owner of the warehouse talked Shawn into taking some Xbox units with some DVD problems to try to learn how to fix. It didn't take long for Shawn to figure out how to do the DVD repairs. In fact, that became our area of expertise. Shawn was so good at DVD repairs that other repair shops started sending us their machines when they got one with a DVD error. We also found with DVD repairs, we had a zero return rate.

Our Xbox repair business made us a lot of money, but it also gave us a lot of stress, mainly because we started doing so many repairs we had to work around the clock. And of course, there was only so much of that we could take before it started to fall apart. I started to watch Shawn break down. We started fighting a lot, and I watched her start to slowly shut down. She'd started journaling again, and one day she left it up on the computer. Upon reading it, I found she had come to a crossroads in her life, not sure of the future and not sure what to do.

She wanted to keep the Xbox repair business going but couldn't do it unless I started handling things better. I felt bad; I knew I kept messing up her life. I wanted to change, I wanted to get better, but no matter what I did it wasn't happening very fast. I realized by reading Shawn's writing she still had hope for me and would stick by me until there was no hope left. She was down, and I knew it was only a matter of time before she lost all hope.

BREAKTHROUGH

June 2009

Shawn

We continued to go to counseling, and I was expecting to start seeing some major changes. But after a few months of counseling and not much change with Justin still having good and bad days, I asked the counselor when my husband would be back to his old self. She looked at me and said, "This *is* your husband. He has suffered a traumatic event, and it has changed him. The only thing we can do is help him deal with it."

I didn't know how to react or what to say. She was telling me, in a way, that the person that I fell in love with and married was gone and would never come back. All I could do was cry and, in a sense, I guess, mourn. I had to accept who my husband was now and that it was not his fault that he had changed.

I found trying to accept Justin was a difficult task. I kept thinking about my dreams that I had sacrificed, and I was bitter. With each passing day, I felt the love I fought so hard to protect slipping away.

I was angry about what I had lost. Over the next few weeks, the target of my anger changed many times. I remembered growing up dreaming of what I thought my husband should be: A man who loved me more than anything, who was a good father and treated his family with respect. I had found the man of my dreams, and now that man was gone.

One day in counseling, Justin was talking about the kids getting on his nerves. He was complaining that they just don't ever listen and that I protected them. He said if I would just let him run the house and the kids like a ship, then everything would be fine. I was trying to understand his anger level, and I said, "Oh, so you get angry with them just being kids, kind of like I get sick of them going, 'Mom! Mom! Mom!' all the time." *BIG* mistake!!! He lost it at that point and started sounding like his anger was just barely under control. I looked over at the counselor to make sense of things for me, and she said I had completely missed what he was saying. He wanted the house to be run like the military because that was what he knew, but it was also part of what kept him feeling safe. When I compared his frustration with the kids with my everyday frustration with them, he felt like I had minimized what he had gone through in the military. I realized then that I wasn't comprehending everything that was going on in his mind.

To me, it just seemed like he carried his experiences with him all the time and never let them go.

A few days later, I called the Vet Center and spoke to our counselor about how I felt. I asked her, "Why can't he just get over it?" We discussed that for a little while, and then she finally asked, "Shawn, knowing all he saw and went through, could you just get over it?" I told her I didn't know, because even though I understand what happened, I couldn't really grasp what the military life was really like because I wasn't there. She suggested I watch the movie *Full Metal Jacket.* She told me to think about myself being one of the characters. Then, hopefully, I would understand where Justin was.

Before hanging up the phone she said, "Shawn, for almost 7 years you've had to deal with Justin's deployment and then him coming home a different person. You've fought so hard to save your family for years alone that it's all you know. You've lost yourself through all of this. When we've talked in sessions, it's always been about helping Justin. We've talked about how you feel with some of the things that have happened, but we haven't really gotten into you having to deal with everything. What you are feeling right now is normal. And you're going to have to go through it before you will accept this. We're to the point now where Justin is okay. We can spend some time on Shawn."

"You're going to have to deal with your emotions now, the ones that you haven't talked about because they are too painful... like when Justin had pulled the gun on you at the house. Not that it wouldn't be scary for anyone it happened to, but it was even more traumatic for you because you knew Justin could do it. You knew his training and that he'd been trained to kill and wouldn't hesitate for a second to do it. So go watch the movie, and then we will start next week with you."

Okay, I thought I'd been dealing with things. I mean, we had to get the gun out of the house so I was no longer scared. The problems were not with me, they were with Justin. But I trusted her and was willing to try whatever she suggested.

So I got the movie *Full Metal Jacket*. Justin asked why I wanted to watch it, and I told him that the counselor thought I needed to see it to understand what military life was like. He chuckled and said, "Oh, you'll see that for sure!" I must have asked him 1,000 times throughout the movie, "Is that what it's really like?" Afterwards, Justin and I sat and talked about the movie and his life in the military. I told him, "I was right. I said it was like you were brainwashed when you went to that antiterrorism training course."

Without realizing it, I was connecting with Justin on a level I never had before. I was beginning to have an understanding why he couldn't "just get over it."

But no matter what deals I tried to make or how angry I was with everyone, nothing was going to bring back the man I married. I knew I had to either accept the man he was now and let go of my dreams or divorce him. I was the only one who could make that decision, and it wasn't going to be easy, but it was a choice I had to make.

Once again I looked back over the time I had been with Justin. I thought about the good times we had together, our children, our house that we made together, and again to the day we got married. Then I tried to imagine life without him. What would it do to the kids, to me? And I wondered, did I really want to start trying to find someone all over again? All I could do was cry and keep crying for days. I knew I just needed to get to the next counseling session and talk to someone about all of this.

Justin

I knew Shawn was hurting, but she wasn't talking to me. As I watched her go through this period I didn't know if she would make it through it. It was like she was finally feeling all of the emotions she should have been feeling the last 7 years.

I wanted to help her, take her pain away, clear any confusion or doubts about me, and just love her. For the first time I realized it wasn't all about me. I had a good woman who loved me with everything she was, even though all those years I treated her like she didn't matter.

I finally accepted I had a problem, and it was called PTSD. I wanted to tell her, "I know now that I can't lose you, I won't stop taking my medicine any more, and I really will change." But I couldn't do it right at that time. She wouldn't believe me; she'd heard it all before, and with her trying to find something to hold on to, saying that might push her away.

I had to let her do this on her own. I felt helpless and could do nothing other than watch and wait. I was so relieved when she called the Vet Center counselor and made an appointment for us to talk. I knew I still had a chance and she wasn't ready to just throw in the towel.

MELTDOWN

June 2009

Shawn

When we walked into our next counseling session, the first thing Justin said was, "She's losing it. I've seen this before, and it ain't good."

I told the counselor how angry I became after watching *Full Metal Jacket*. We talked about the military and the VA for a while, and then she wanted to talk about things from the beginning. I didn't really see how that was going to help and was resistant to talking about it.

She asked about how I handled Justin's deployment. I told her I was fine. I had missed him, but I dealt with things just fine. I mean Justin was in the Navy; you get use to them being gone for six months at a time. So us being at war didn't put that much of a strain on us. The only thing I resented was that we didn't get to have the nice church wedding I had planned. Not only was the date we had planned shot down by his deployment, but I let his mom convince me Justin and I would have lots more money because he would get paid more for us being married. If we eloped, that money would start sooner. But deep down, I kept looking at all those bride magazines I had bought and felt cheated out of something nice. Other than that, though, I had gotten used to him being gone for long periods of time. The last deployment was the hardest on us because I was pregnant, was emotional, and felt like I was having to do it all by myself. But I understood that it wasn't his fault.

I knew what was coming next, but I was not ready to talk about it. "How about when Justin came home?" she asked. *What did she expect me to say? It was hard.* She told me to dig deep and really just let it out.

I once again avoided it by telling her, "We're here about Justin, not me."

We argued about talking about me for a few moments until she finally said, "Shawn, for years you've fought to save your marriage, don't stop now when you're so close. You are what is holding it back now. Until you face your emotions, this marriage will not be whole."

Part of me knew she was right, but I just didn't think I could talk about it. It wasn't just that I wasn't used to talking about my feelings, it's that living with Justin had taught me I *shouldn't* talk about my true feelings. If I was angry or upset about something, one of two things would happen. Either Justin would become *furious*, supposedly on my behalf but really in a way that made it more about him. Or, he would say things that invalidated my feelings. He would compare my pain from a kidney stone to a cut on his leg or try to get in a contest about who worked harder. He always made sure I knew he was the more miserable one between us. I had gotten to the point where I never opened my mouth when something was wrong, and it felt strange to try to do it now.

As resistant I was, I started to talk. But once I started, I couldn't stop. "I thought when Justin came home we would be this happy family. But we weren't. I was pregnant, and he wouldn't even look at me. And I couldn't even touch him without him freaking out if he didn't see it coming. I tried to deal with those things, so I figured he just needed some time to adjust to being back home.

"Then he wouldn't unpack his bags, he would pull these disappearing acts, and he didn't help out with the baby, so I felt like he would rather be back on the ship. I thought I could help him through things. But he shoved me away and wouldn't talk to me other than to yell at me. Somehow, everything became my fault, even if I had nothing to do with what he was angry about. I felt like he wasn't attracted to me because I found out he would rather watch porn than touch me.

"It's like he would rather be back in the military than be here with his family. It's like he was lost without being on his ship. I tried to love him enough, but I found out no amount of love would fix him. Even just talking to him could get him into a rage. He got so angry about stuff that didn't even pertain to us. The kid across the street got in trouble for selling weed, and I was just trying to tell him about it, which was a mistake because he started going off about how if the kid came over in our yard he would get shot. You couldn't explain to him that his thought process wasn't right and that you couldn't do those things. He always came back with, 'Civilians need to be treated just like in the military. That will stop all this stupid crap,' or, 'Drugs are how the terrorists get money to keep their operations going.' His mind is 24/7 in military mode and always watching out like he is forever at war.

"And what's worse, he's dragged me into this war mindset with him. I play *Call of Duty 4* and *Gears of War*, but I don't just *play* them, I really *get into* those stupid games."

"Okay, when you tried to help Justin through things and it didn't work, how did you feel?" she asked.

"What do you mean how did I feel?!?" I asked. "I felt worthless! I couldn't deal with it. I would have rather been dead than keep living the way we were going. Hell, I didn't just *think* I would rather be dead; I attempted it on more than one occasion."

"Why did you try to kill yourself? What did you do? Why didn't you just leave? If you were that miserable, why didn't you divorce him and be done with all of it?" the counselor asked.

I remember thinking, *Why do I have to sit here pouring out my heart and soul?* I glanced over at Justin who was just sitting there with that blank emotionless thousand-yard stare I had come to hate.

I looked back down shaking my head trying to fight back the tears. "What does it matter? He doesn't care anyway." I mumbled.

Then out of nowhere, I felt Justin's hand on my shoulder. I looked over at him, and he told me, "Just tell her. Tell her everything."

I couldn't tell you exactly how I felt at that moment, but I remember saying, "Oh well... What the hell?" Then I took a deep breath and regained my composure the best I could before I continued speaking.

"Why did I try to kill myself? Let's go through all the many reasons," I said with a smart-ass attitude. I guess trying to be cocky about the whole thing was my attempt to keep it together and not let my emotions get the best of me.

But as I began to speak about everything, fighting back the emotions proved to be a difficult task.

"The first time was probably about six months after Justin returned home. Things weren't going well between us, as you know. I felt unloved and unwanted, and then Justin informed me that his mother thought it would be best if we got a divorce. Completely out of nowhere, they blindsided me with this. Because with my kidneys and all of the medical bills piling up, she told Justin that if he divorced me, then if something happened to me they couldn't come after him for the money. I was hurt, and the fact that Justin even told me about this meant he must be okay with it and that our marriage was nothing to him. I told him he could have his divorce and that I would move out with the kids, and he got ugly and told me I would never get custody of the kids. Not wanting to put the kids through hell, I said fine, that I wouldn't fight it and went back to the bedroom, locked the door, grabbed the gun, and put it in my mouth. I was going to do it because I didn't feel like my life mattered to anyone. But Justin kicked in the door and got the gun away from me. We talked, and I cried, and he said he wouldn't divorce me. It wasn't worth all of this just to get away from paying medical bills."

"So, that was the first time."

I looked up at Justin then, and he was nodding his head agreeing with what I was saying. So I look back at the counselor and continued.

"The second time was around the time he sent me flying across the kitchen and the cops were called. I just couldn't take living with someone who didn't give a shit about me, and no one would listen to me or help me with Justin, so I saw no other way out. But once again Justin stopped me and this time got me into counseling. They decided I had postpartum depression.

"They put me on some meds, which didn't really work and made things worse, so they switched them around until they found one that worked.

"The problem that caused was that it validated in Justin's mind that I was the one with the issues, not him, and it gave him ammo against me any time I threatened to leave. So leaving, then, was no longer an option because the minute I said anything about taking the kids, he was quick to remind me that the suicide attempts were on paper and that no one would allow the kids to be with me. So what was I supposed to do? I mean I had no one, really. I had distanced myself from my family and friends. I hadn't talked to them about anything that had been going on because it was my marriage and we didn't need anyone else involved with it and also because my mom had already said something about me being emotionally abused and that would just give her more reason to think that I really was being abused. I didn't have a job. My life revolved around Justin, the kids, and our home, so it wasn't like I had any way of making it on my own. And Justin had his whole family lined up against me. His mom hated me, and his dad despised me all because any time we would fight, Justin would run to them and tell them how bad I was. So really, what was I supposed to do?"

The room was silent for a moment. I threw my hands up in the air and shrugged my shoulders as if to say, "I give up! I'm cornered, and someone really needs to tell me my next move because I don't know what it is."

The counselor looked at Justin and then at me and asked, "So what is it that you want? You feel trapped, unwanted, unloved, and emotionally beat down. You have no one to talk to, and I'm guessing you're basically a slave to this life and a man who's changed and isn't the man you married. Am I right? So, where do you want things to go from here? Do you want a divorce, do you just want to separate for a while, or do you want to try and fix this?"

At that moment my jaw dropped and I shot the counselor the look of, *Are you kidding me?!?* I then looked over at Justin to find him staring at me with that stupid, emotionless stare he does while waiting for my reply.

I shrugged my shoulders, shook my head, and replied, "I don't know. I just don't know. I've got to think about the kids and if it's better for them to go through a divorce or continue living in a house that is absolute hell. I want to think it's going to get better and that this is something that we can work through, but you've pretty much said Justin has changed and that this is who he is now. So does that mean that it's going to be miserable for the rest of our lives? Does it mean that I have to settle for feeling alone because he no longer has emotions? I need to know what is in store for us as far as will Justin ever get back to being the man I married?

"Then I also have my own beliefs to consider. I believe you only marry once. When I said, 'Till death do us part,' I meant it! You have to tell me, because right now I can't say what I want. I know what I want or hope that will happen, but is that even a reality?

"And I'm angry right now. I know this isn't Justin's fault, but then who do I blame? Who can I take out my frustration on?"

I looked over at Justin hoping that for once he would be a man and tell me that he loved me and wanted our marriage to work. But he quickly turned his head, looking down at the floor, once again leaving me to feel like he didn't care. I rolled my eyes and looked towards the window shaking my head thinking that that was it. He'd just proved to me our marriage was over.

At that point the counselor could tell we were done. There was an uncomfortable silence, and neither Justin nor I had anything else to say. I looked over at the clock thinking, or maybe hoping, our time was up. The counselor told me that we still had some time and that there were just a few more things we needed to discuss.

I was spent and didn't want to be there any longer, but I figured we might as well go ahead and finish this so we could just be done. So I nodded my head to agree but continued looking out the window. The counselor then asked me who I was mad at and why.

I sat there for just a moment thinking, and then I looked at her and replied, "I don't know who I am mad at. I am mad at a lot of things. I am mad at the military for brainwashing my husband and then not changing him back. It was like they reprogrammed his brain. They broke him down through fear until he stopped reacting with his emotions. They beat it into his head that if he let his guard down for a second, he could be killed. They knew what they were doing to get the results they wanted.

"When he left the training, they had him so keyed up that when all these things happened it fried his brain. Then without deprogramming him, they just shipped him back to me with no warning about what I would have to deal with. And then for allowing the things that happened that caused his PTSD."

The counselor stopped me and asked what I was talking about.

I told her, "Between the training classes they sent him to and the boat coming straight at his ship on his last deployment, when they ordered him to not do anything, it got him so freaked out he snapped."

"Shawn, Justin's PTSD is caused by a combination of different things; you know that. The plane crash, the dead bodies, and the incident with the boat *all* caused his PTSD." replied the counselor.

I looked at her with confusion and told her, "The plane crash and the dead bodies were accidents that weren't anyone's fault; they may or may not have caused him to have severe PTSD. But the incident with the boat... They could have let him fire a warning shot to scare them off. Maybe then he wouldn't have freaked out."

She then tried to explain to me that he couldn't just fire a warning shot without being ordered to do so. I understood what she was saying, but the commanding officer wasn't the one whose ass was on the line. We kept going back and forth with her trying to explain to me that there were rules that had to be followed and me asking her why. I didn't understand. We were at war! How could they not be able to defend themselves and have to wait for orders if they felt they were in danger? Finally she just said, "It's the Geneva Convention."

Well that stopped me dead in my tracks. I knew what that was, but those rules didn't apply when you were defending yourself. The Geneva Convention laid out a guideline on treatment of POWs and civilians. It said you can't attack hospitals or medics and can't destroy national landmarks and that military forces must have something to identify them as soldiers. The counselor agreed, but explained there were other rules our military had to follow.

I thought about it for a second and then asked her, "You're talking about standard rules of engagement, right? Where we can use necessary force for self-defense in response to a hostile act or demonstrated hostile intent during peace time? The upper military and government put these rules out to protect our troops and to make sure there left no doubt that they were being attacked. The whole *Top Gun* thing: do not fire until fired upon."

She said I was right to a point, but there was a lot more to it. Those rules also applied to war time along with the Geneva Convention rules. That the enemy had to do something that was hostile before we could do anything. This was crazy! Our enemy didn't follow any rules! What happened to the USS Cole proved that. There was nothing hostile about that situation.

So I asked her, "You mean to tell me that these enemies wear no uniforms, represent terrorist cells instead of governments, observe no rules, and use women and children to attack our military, and now our government has set guidelines on our military to protect civilians that have exceeded the basic standards of The Geneva Conventions? Those standards were created during WWII before terrorists like this even existed, and they weren't written for this type of warfare. These new rules can jeopardize our soldiers' safety in combat zones because they are more concerned with being 'Politically Correct.' What the hell are they supposed to do, let them shoot and hope they miss before they can do anything?!? No wonder so many are coming home with PTSD! This is insane!"

She told me that they weren't rules designed to tie our military's hands. It was meant to protect innocent people from getting killed. I thought, *Yeah, whatever. They would rather our military get killed then accidently kill some civilians that may have been posing a threat.* She could tell I was frustrated and changed the subject by asking if there was anyone who I was angry with.

I said, "Yeah, there is a part of me that's mad at God because I don't know what I did to deserve this. He could have stopped this from happening to Justin, but he didn't. I'd stuck by my husband. I was faithful in my marriage. So why was this happening? Now I was supposed to live the rest of my life with someone who was nothing like the man I married? I didn't sign up for this. Why should I have to stay in this marriage?

"I remember one night yelling at God. I even tried making a deal with God, if he would just bring my husband back, then I would be a better Christian woman.

"I'm mad at the government and the VA for not doing anything. They turned their heads and acted like they didn't know what was going on when they really did. This government, our government, wouldn't help him after he served them. They used him for what they needed and then threw him aside. They turned us away the first two times that I called for help. They knew about all of this. Many veterans had returned home with the same problems, and when I called, they kept silent. It wasn't until the suicide rate had become an epidemic that they decided to do anything. When I called the VA for help they didn't even tell me about the Vet Centers.

"And I guess there is a part of me that's mad at Justin. I remember thinking, *Just deal with it already! It's part of life! It sucks, I know, but get over it!* I know that seems cruel, but I had to blame someone. I'm mad he won't talk to me, that he treats me and the kids the way he does, and that he turned his back on our marriage. I know he doesn't mean to, but I can't help but want to make him feel like I do. I want him to understand and see what he has done to me and the kids."

I felt bad for saying that, but it was how I felt. A part of me wanted to make him pay for the hell he'd put me through. Out of the corner of my eye, I could see Justin. He was still looking at the floor, but I could tell by his expression on his face that he was angry. I didn't know if he was angry at what I'd just said or if he was just angry at the whole situation. At that moment, I didn't really care who or what he was angry at. But then I noticed his facial expression wasn't angry. It looked that way because he was trying to fight back the tears.

Seeing his face broke my heart and I wanted to make it stop for him. I knew the only way to do that was to finish what we had already started. I had to keep going and get it all out.

So I looked up at the ceiling and through the lump in my throat I continued talking. "But most of all, I'm mad at me. I'm mad that I wasn't a better wife who made him feel safe enough to trust and confide in. I'm mad that I wasn't understanding and pushed him to his limits, and I'm mad that I never took the time to try to understand what he went through while in the military. But over the last few weeks I understand now. I get it now."

Finally, it was out. As I looked up at Justin with eyes full of tears, I told him, "I'm sorry. I'm sorry I didn't understand what you went through."

He never said a word, but he reached over and put his arm around me holding me tight. I started crying even harder and when I put my arms around him, I looked up and said, "Finally." Justin started to laugh, which made me laugh, and for that moment we were connected emotionally again.

I then turned my head towards the counselor and asked, "So what's next?"

She couldn't help but smile and then replied, "This was good. You needed to get this out. There is still a long road ahead, and it won't always be easy, but what happens next is still in your hands. Shawn you need to find a way to accept who Justin is now, and Justin you need to make sure you're committed to getting help and doing your part with counseling and medication. So go home and talk about things. Shawn, continue to write in your journal. It will help more than you know. And Justin, when you've been upset or in a rage, I want you to take these papers and fill them out after you've calmed down. Write what you are upset about, what triggered it, what calmed you down, and how you felt. And then next week both of you bring in what you wrote down, and we will discuss them at that time."

So Justin and I got up to leave. Both of us were very happy at that point. But as I was starting to walk out the door, the counselor grabbed my arm and told me, "I mean it, you either have to accept him for who he is now or walk away. You make a clean break, or you start new today. You can't keep throwing everything he has done in the past in his face. I don't want to see y'all divorced, but no one will blame you if that's the decision that you make. Right now you feel good and feel like a huge burden has been lifted, but believe me when I say: With PTSD, you never know when it will rear its ugly head.

"Justin loves you; he would've never gotten rid of the gun if he didn't care. But you also need to be ready to practice tough love if you decide to stay. He's going to have to learn to control his temper, or you're going to have to be ready to call the cops when he is being physically destructive. You and the kids do not need to live with that. What happened before is in the past. He knows right and wrong now, and he has to learn there are consequences for his actions."

I nodded my head to let her know I understood

and turned to leave. Although I was still happy that Justin had finally shown just a little bit of emotion, what she said to me brought me back down to reality, and I had some decisions to make that were not going to be easy.

Justin

Sitting there listening to her, I felt like the biggest asshole in the world. I knew I had caused her pain, but to sit there and listen to it all coming out of her mouth and to see her face was almost unbearable. I had almost destroyed the person I loved.

When I started dating Shawn, she was a strong woman that could do anything she set her mind to. She went to church, was a single parent, had a good job, and was full of life. She didn't need *anyone* to take care of her because she was so independent. But now she was a different woman, and whether I meant to or not, I was responsible for her current state. I beat her down emotionally, controlled her, and made her this shell of a person that had been shattered. I wanted to take it all back, take her pain away, but I couldn't.

I heard what the counselor said. This was going to be very hard for me. I mean, I was just learning about my triggers and trying to learn how to control my temper. One outburst, and she could send me to jail. But it was all a process and it took time. I had only barely figured out that part of my addiction to porn and relationships with online women was because when I first came home, I didn't feel emotionally connected to Shawn or even trust her enough to get physically closer. I considered just going ahead and leaving. But after all the pain I'd already caused, I decided to leave the decision up to her and work my hardest on making things right. Whatever happened from this point out I deserved.

DETERMINATION

June 2009 — August 2009

Shawn

Once again I was stuck making the hardest decision of my life. So I decided to look back over the last 7 years with Justin. I started reading my journal, and for the first time I actually saw a pattern to what I was doing. I hadn't quite realized as I was living through it all that from the time Justin came home, I had started the five steps of grieving.

My denial stage started with thinking Justin was just having a hard time adjusting. I kept thinking, *He'll get better*, never really letting myself see the truth, which was that the man I fell in love with, that was the grown-up version of that sweet, protective little boy, was forever lost to me. No matter what happened from that point forward, he would forever be affected by his experiences in the service.

I did stages two and three out of order from how they usually happen. The bargaining stage began when I started walking on eggshells. Somewhere in the back of my head I must have been thinking that if I was *good enough* and did all the right things, everything would go back to how it used to be.

I was stalled at this point for years. Writing became my outlet, how I kept my own sanity. It was my way of talking to someone, even if it was just to me. It also allowed me a way to open the lines of communication once we began counseling. Each day we would write about things that happened and then discuss them in counseling.

The last three stages in the grieving process—anger, depression, and acceptance—came rather quickly once I allowed them to. But I did flip back and forth between them a few times.

At that point, I grabbed my headphones and started to speak about what I was reading and understanding in my journal. I wanted to make sure I had this written down so I could see it in black and white. I wasn't any good with a pen and paper; I never could write what I really felt. But this way I would just say what I was thinking or feeling and it would automatically put my words onto paper on the computer. So I went back and started with the first stage of grieving.

1.Denial – Alright, when I was thinking Justin was having a hard time adjusting to being home I was in denial.

2.Anger – Looks like I flirted with anger off and on but never truly hit it until Justin was finally in counseling and I was trying to understand it all. Almost 5 years since Justin came home before I really hit the second stage in grieving.

3.Bargaining – I bargained by trying to walk on eggshells, making excuses for his actions thinking it would make him stop and thinking if I loved him enough he would change. But I went into full blown bargaining at the same time that I hit the anger stage and tried making a deal with God.

4.Depression – Hmmm. I had hit this stage a long time ago. This one had been present all along. I felt hopeless, I felt alone, I flirted with suicide, I felt numb, and I saw no way out.

5.Acceptance – I'm here right now. In counseling the other day, I finally dealt with everything else. I'm at a crossroads, and I know I have to choose. But I do have a choice in this.

I sat there staring at the screen. I didn't know what to think of my new revelation. What exactly did this mean for me? That all along I knew that the man I married was gone and just didn't realize that I knew? How could I not have known? Or is it that I just didn't want to see it?

I was stuck again, but I knew questioning myself was not getting me anywhere. I sat and looked at the journal and the books I had gotten on PTSD. I was hoping the answer would just pop out at me, that I would have some sign as to what I was supposed to do. But none of this was getting me any closer to making a lifelong decision. I mean it shouldn't be that hard. Either I was willing to stay and accept all the crap that comes along with Justin and his PTSD, or I would have to leave and start all over again without all the crap.

The more I looked for an answer, the more frustrated I was becoming. But then I got a nice and unexpected distraction. I heard my little ones laughing as they came in the door. It immediately put a smile on my face, and I jumped up to go see them. When I got to the front room, the kids were getting their clothes in a bag and yelling for daddy to wait for them. They saw me standing there and told me to hurry up because Daddy was taking us camping. I smiled and said okay as they ran out the door.

I watched out the window as Jaxson ran towards Justin with his arms raised so his daddy would pick him up. I knew right then that was my sign, the answer I had searched for everywhere. Leaving was not an option. It didn't matter what Justin had said or done in the past. My son had just shown me that his daddy was still the same person deep inside and that all that mattered was staying together and fixing our problems as a family.

I would stay.

Justin

I tried to leave Shawn alone for a few days after she lost it big time in counseling so she could process what had happened. I tried to not do or say anything to upset her. In fact, I hardly said anything at all.

I planned a camping trip with the kids to give her some time to herself. I got the truck all loaded and told the kids to get their stuff together. Next thing I knew, Shawn was coming out the door to go with us. I told her that she didn't have to and that I was taking the kids so she could have some time alone, but she said she didn't need it, that she wanted to be with the family.

I wasn't sure how to take that, and I didn't want to assume that meant she had made a decision about staying. But late one night by the campfire, she told me that she had decided to stay as long as I was willing to go to counseling and treat her better than I had been treating her before. She made it very clear what she would and wouldn't tolerate. I told her I was willing to do all that, and I was *very* happy to hear she was staying. I tried to show her that later on in the tent. I wasn't trying to push my luck, but I wanted to show her my appreciation.

VA

August 2009 — August 2010

Shawn

We knew the counselor's time as an intern was up, but Justin wasn't dealing with her leaving very well. In August 2009, while in one of our last counseling sessions, she was explaining to us that the new therapist they were putting Justin with had a background in family counseling. When she asked Justin if he was okay with all of this, he replied, "What does it matter? I've already been going here the six months that I was told I had to go to counseling."

The therapist and I looked at each other, both of us shocked. She told Justin, "You don't have to come here if you don't want to be here. If these sessions aren't helping you, then you don't have to come."

I immediately jumped in and asked, "Who said you only have to come here six months?"

"The guy I talked to the first day down at the VA. He said I would only need to come here for six months," replied Justin.

I threw my hands up, and the therapist held her finger up to tell me to wait a minute. She looked at Justin and asked him, "Do you think you need counseling? Is it helping you at all? Do you think you and your family will be okay without counseling?"

Justin sat there for a moment, then nodded his head yes and agreed that he did need counseling. He also apologized and said he was just stressed out and having a bad day.

At the end of the session we said our good-byes, and she told us that the new counselor would be there taking patients in about 2 weeks. The problem came when the new therapist didn't start working in 2 weeks like they originally said she would. Two weeks turned into 2 months; and 2 months turned into 6 months. During that 6 months we were waiting for the new counselor, things between Justin and I got very tense.

Our Xbox 360 repair business was going very well. We were making enough money that Justin and I both were able to work from home. But in August, Justin ripped a muscle in his leg. We ended up in the ER, and they gave him some medicine for pain. Three days later he ended up back in the ER with 104 degree temperature. They admitted him late on Friday night and started running tests. Come to find out by Sunday, he had somehow gotten the "MRSA superbug," which they described to me as a combination of both the hospital variety MRSA staph infection and the community MRSA. Aside from his high fever, the infection had seated itself in his injured leg muscle to the point where he could barely walk. The strain he had was drug resistant, but they still were trying various medications.

Because Justin got so bad on the weekend, the VA didn't get word he was sick until that Monday. That day the VA said Justin had to be transferred to a VA hospital, which was alright... other than the closest one was over an hour away and I couldn't find anyone to watch the kids! My family and Justin's family all had to work, and Paula was going out of town for three days. I hated it that Justin was going to have to go by himself, and I was angry about it being so far away. But then as we were waiting for them to pick Justin up, they called back to let us know we had to go to the St. Louis VA hospital, which was 3 hours away and that Justin had to find his own way since his disability had not been decided and he wasn't considered a disabled vet.

We waited to leave until Justin had received his IV medicine and I had the kids lined up as to where they were staying. Justin was in excruciating agony for the 3 hours we spent driving because they had sent him with no pain medication. I wanted to drive faster to get there sooner, but he felt every bump in the road as it was, so I tried to be careful. By the time we got to the VA hospital, it was about 1:00 a.m.

When we arrived a nurse took us to a room and started Justin's IV. After the nurse was finished, he looked at me and said I needed to leave. *What? Where was I going to go?* I explained to him that we were 3 hours away from our home, that I had no money for a hotel, and that I wasn't *about* to leave my husband when I had worked so hard to arrange for someone to watch the kids so I could be there.

At that point, the floor nurse came in, and they told me I couldn't stay in the room with Justin because it wasn't a private room. I told them I didn't care; I would be sleeping in a chair right next to Justin. They explained to me that it was against policy since Justin wasn't in a private room. When they told me they had a family room I could stay in, I immediately told them we were leaving. The nurse chased me down the hall telling me that was the worst thing I could do for Justin. When I looked at my husband, I saw he was in so much pain that I knew he couldn't be moved. So I agreed to stay in the family room.

They stuck me in a room with six strange men. When I told them I wasn't comfortable with that, they said, "We're not here to make spouses comfortable. We're here to take care of the veteran." I think I slept with one eye open all night.

When I got back up to Justin's room, he was still in a lot of pain. I demanded to see the doctor who came in, and instead of speaking to me, he started talking to the nurse. I immediately stopped the doctor and told him that he needed to be talking to me and explaining what was going on. He apologized and then told me they needed to figure out how Justin got this particular type of MRSA since he had no open wounds, which is how MRSA gets in, so they were going to do some tests and get him some pain medicine.

While sitting there waiting for Justin to get back from his tests, I started noticing how disgusting Justin's room looked. Paint was peeling off the walls, there were cracks in the walls and ceiling, and the lockers in the room were rusted. I picked up the phone and started calling all our parents and telling them about it. The tests eventually showed that he had probably gotten it from some bloodwork at the other hospital when he first injured his leg muscle, but there was no way to know for sure.

My mom told me conditions like that were the norm at all the VA hospitals. She said, "They look awful and run down, but you will get the best care there," which she would know from taking my grandpa to his VA appointments. So I let it go and waited for Justin to get back from his test.

When he returned the pain medicine had kicked in, and he was feeling much better. So I decided that I would go ahead and tell him that I was going home that night. I told him I just couldn't sleep in a room with a bunch of guys I didn't know, and I had Xbox 360 consoles that were already sold that I needed to get out. Later that night when it was time to leave, I tried to cheer Justin up by telling him I would be back first thing in the morning. I could tell by the tears in his eyes he didn't want me to go. I think I cried the first hour I was driving. I hated that he was upset. I knew when I was sick and in the hospital, I didn't want him to leave me.

It was about midnight when I got home, and I knew I only had four hours to work on Xbox 360 consoles before I would have to leave again to get back up to the hospital first thing in the morning. I did this for five days every day and only slept when Justin did during the day. I have never been so tired in my life. However, it all seemed worth it to me because I could see Justin improving day by day. That doctor may not have been the best communicator, and the hospital may not have looked that great, but the way that doctor and his staff cared for Justin, I couldn't have asked for more. By day five, I was hugging the nurses, thanking them, and apologizing for yelling at them... although I still think they needed a better way to care for spouses staying there to support the patients.

When Justin was released from the hospital, he had to be given medicine twice a day and stayed on pain medication for a few weeks, so he was no help to me. I was trying to fix the consoles, ship them out, and handle all the ones that were returned to us broken. It was all too much for me to handle. So once the last Xbox 360 unit was sold, I never got anymore.

Justin

When it came time for my therapist at the Vet Center to leave, I wasn't really concerned with going back after that. It was hard for me to want to go through a new therapist and re-explaining everything that happened again. Plus the new counselor wasn't a veteran, so I didn't think she could relate or understand what I was going through. But counseling was helping, and Shawn's and my relationship was improving, so I knew I needed to continue going. During the time I was waiting for the new therapist to get there, I ended up getting deathly ill with a staph infection that would bring our Xbox repair business to a complete halt. Shawn drove 3 hours to see me at the VA hospital, and when visiting hours were over, she drove 3 hours back home, worked all night on fixing Xbox 360 consoles, got them ready to be shipped out, and then turned around and did it again. She did this every day for over a week. I couldn't believe she was doing all of this for me! I would have never gone to those extremes for Shawn if she was sick.

When I got sent home, I had a PIC line (permanently installed central catheter) and had to get medicine twice a day. Shawn had to do all of that, plus deal with all the complaints and returned Xbox machines. I knew it was too much for her to deal with. She was overwhelmed, overworked, and exhausted, but she still tried to stay strong for me. I knew I needed to get us back to the Vet Center as soon as I had the strength to do so for Shawn's sake.

She needed to talk to someone and maybe get some advice on how to handle everything going on, if for nothing else, to be able to vent and release some of the weight she was carrying on her shoulders. I wanted her to see that I realized how much she loved me. I wanted to take care of her, and for the first time, I really understood how bad I had treated her over the years. Hell, it would have served me right for her to drop me on my ass as pay back for the way I treated her all that time. It was amazing; I was falling in love all over again with my wife. I actually was feeling something, which I had not been able to do for a long time.

Shawn

Once Justin started to feel better, I started to think about what we would do for money. But then in October 2009 I received a letter from the VA requesting additional information on Justin's disability claim and saying if they didn't receive the information, they might make a decision on the claim based on the information they already had at the time. I thought to myself, *Wow, this is moving quickly!* We had heard it can take years for a disability claim to go through. So I started cruising the internet to find out what I needed to do when submitting additional information.

I discovered that since Justin didn't have a "Combat MOS," a Purple Heart, a Combat Infantry Badge, or a medal for valor, they wanted something called a stressor letter. This letter was supposed to prove that Justin had experienced a traumatic event strong enough to produce PTSD.

For the next week I found out everything I could on writing a stressor letter and learning all about the disability claims process. The first thing I learned about stressor letters was that they have to be broken down into three vital parts. The first section needed to cover life before service. The second would cover life during the service including the traumatic events. And the third section would cover how life has changed since the events causing PTSD. Each of those sections were very important to the VA so they could get an understanding how the stressors effected Justin personally. So we would need to enclose a very detailed account of the traumatic events, as well as his personal triggers that would produce any flashbacks, anxiety attacks, anger, and nightmares. All of this, if not done correctly, could get his claim denied immediately. It was also best if family members submitted a letter, so I knew I would have to write a letter about what changes I saw in Justin. I also learned we had one year from the date we filed Justin's disability claim to submit the additional information. So I decided to put it off for a while and go back to figuring out how to get money coming back into the house, since gathering all the information may take some time.

Justin was supportive of what I was doing, but the fact that I was spending all my time trying to work from home caused a lot of problems and fights between the two of us. Since it was too much of a hassle for us to continue fixing Xbox consoles, I decided to write a book about how to repair the units and sell that, but I needed a lot of time to myself to concentrate on the book. That left Justin trying to watch the kids, cook for them, and (attempt to) clean the house, and he had a low tolerance for that. I guess he didn't like being Mr. Mom. I was so glad in November when he could see the new therapist at the Vet Center.

Justin

When we got the letter from the VA, I knew I couldn't do anything. Shawn is really good at handling things like that, so I just let her. When she started telling me about writing a stressor letter, I told her, "You know my story, so just write it." She told me she would help me, but they needed to know how I felt when the traumatic events happened, so it needed to be my words. I couldn't do that and I knew like everything else, Shawn would take care of it for me.

When Shawn started working on her new angle for working at home, I was excited for her. I just didn't realize how much work was going to go into it between writing the book and taking photographs of all the repair steps. I had to take care of the kids while she worked on it, which was something I wasn't used to. When I first started with the new therapist at the Vet Center, Shawn didn't even go to the sessions with me because she was always working. I thought when she got things going in December that life would be great and would go back to the way they were before this book.

Shawn

Justin thought things were going to go back to the way they were, but we quickly found out that working from home required a lot more time than we ever imagined. In January 2010, I got another letter from the VA requesting additional information. This time, though, it said that if the information wasn't received they would make a decision on the case without it. I knew I needed to work on Justin's stressor letter, write my letter to the VA, and still spend time on my work-from-home stuff. So every day for the next two months I spent time working on all of it. Justin's letter was not the easiest to get done. He was being very difficult when I had questions about anything with his military service. It took me a few months to do, but when finished the letter looked like this:

Life Before Military Service

I was born on November 25, 1981 in Evansville, Indiana. I am my mother's first child and my dad's second child. My childhood seemed normal and carefree to me, even though my parents divorced when I was a baby. In elementary school, I performed well academically and joined and participated in the Boy Scouts. I had a few close friends during that time, and we spent much of our time playing many different sports. I also had a few hobbies during those formative years. For instance, I collected baseball cards and toy soldiers. I was never sick, never had any broken bones, and was pretty much healthy.

By high school, I found girls were more on my mind then studying. I got in what I would call, "normal teenage trouble." One time I snuck out and took off on my step-dad's motor scooter just to impress a girl. Or I would stay up late at night talking to a girl on the phone. Nothing very bad, but my grades suffered dearly for it. I also worked at Denny's during high school so I could buy a car, and in the summer my best friend and I started our own lawn mowing business. When it came time to graduate, I had no clue what I wanted to do with my life. My family didn't think college was for me and started talking to me about going into the military. Right before graduation in June 2000, I enlisted in the Navy.

LIFE DURING MILITARY SERVICE

In June 2000, I was sent to Chicago, Illinois, for boot camp. It went by pretty quickly, and I was trained to be a Machinist Mate. After boot camp, I received my orders to the USS George Washington CVN-73, so I was put on a plane to go overseas where the Washington was finishing up a tour in the Middle East. The first year and a half of service was pretty easy going and laid back. I cross-rated in the summer of 2001 to an Operation Specialist because I saw no chance for advancement as a Machinist Mate.

On September 11, 2001, I was in the control room of the USS George Washington when the attacks on the United States happened. I was angry and ready to go attack whoever was responsible for the destruction they caused. In June 2002, we were deployed to aid in Operation Enduring Freedom. We saw no action during that deployment and even were treated to a concert by 3 Doors Down aboard our ship.

During that deployment, I was pulled over to be Military Police. I really enjoyed that position and felt that I had found my home there. On February 4, 2003 we responded to a distress call from the Coast Guard. Four survivors were rescued, and one person died of hypothermia. The small fishing vessel they were on had caught fire. I was responsible for securing the body of the deceased while the other four were treated on board the ship. This was the first time I had ever handled a dead body.

When we returned to the United States, I was sent for an anti-terrorism training course. It was intense. In the classroom we talked a lot about what happened to the USS Cole and watched a lot of videos showing the aftermath. They taught us about how terrorists can use many different things to make a bomb and how easy it is for terrorists to sneak bombs into just about anywhere. I took my training very seriously, and at the end I was promoted to the Rapid Response Team Leader.

On September 11, 2003, during an F/18 arrested landing, the arresting gear cable snapped back across the deck of the USS George Washington injuring several crew members. I immediately ran up to the flight deck and started making routes and blocking off areas so the injured could be treated. I didn't care who you were; no one was getting past me unless they were medics or injured. I then had to help keep the injured crew members calm. I had to tell them they would be alright, even if I didn't think they were.

When it was over I couldn't get the whole thing out of my head. I just wanted to forget it happened, but when I closed my eyes I could see it again. And each time more and more people were injured. I couldn't help them all.

In November 2003 a crew member on the ship was killed when a fuel tank fell from the belly of the plane he was working on and crushed him. I was in charge so I had to secure the body and keep people away. I had my team build a wall so no one could see when they lifted the fuel tank and his body was exposed. To see him after they removed the fuel tank shook me to my core. I thought about the fishing boat we rescued and the body of the one person who died that I had to handle. I thought about the plane crash and realized right then that at any moment it could be any of us laying here dead.

In January 2004 we were deployed again in support of OEF/OIF. While we were making our transit through the Suez Canal, I was on watch when I noticed a small boat heading straight for us. I called it in to the bridge and was told to keep watch on the boat. So I never took my eyes off of it, all the while thinking about my training and about what happened to the USS Cole. They were still coming, so I locked and loaded. I took aim at the boat and called the bridge again asking for the go ahead to fire a warning shot. I was told to stand my ground and keep watching them. My heart was pounding; I had never been so scared and pumped up at the same time in my life. Then I watched the boat suddenly change directions. I informed the bridge of the change in direction and fell back into the chair. That one was too close. I could actually see myself as one of the injured, like in the plane crash or one of the dead bodies lying there that I had to handle.

In June 2004, I was flown off the USS George Washington and headed to Norfolk to be processed out of the military.

LIFE SINCE THE TRAUMATIC EVENTS

Since returning home, adjusting to civilian life has been extremely difficult. I quickly realized that home is not what I thought it would be. For 4 years I was told what to do and when to do it. I wasn't exactly sure what I was supposed to do. I tried finding a job, but not many places were hiring. So took whatever jobs I could. I was having nightmares and even attacked my wife in my sleep. I didn't want to deal with people and avoided it at all cost. I was angry about everything and had a lot of rage.

My wife and I have had a lot of trouble since I returned home. I don't feel emotions like she does. I am not close to my kids at all. In fact I can't handle being around them very much without getting angry. I have had nine jobs in 4 years and been fired from six of those. When I am not working, I would rather be by myself. I have pulled a gun on my wife, punched holes in walls, and destroyed my house in a rage.

I have been in counseling for a year now at the VA and the Vet Center. I attend weekly therapy sessions, and I am on many medicines to help me cope with life.

I was very happy with the stressor letter. Now I just needed Justin to look over it and then rewrite it so I could send it in to the VA. I knew it would take him some time to do that, so I didn't push. But it seemed like reading that triggered Justin in some way.

I started going to his Vet Center appointments with him. I met his new counselor and explained to her that since he read the stressor letter, he had been having nightmares again and was very agitated. She called the VA and got him back in to see his doctor at the VA. When we went to his VA appointment, the doctor wanted to add Paxil to his list of medicines. It was the normal 15-minute appointment with orders to come back in 3 months for a med check.

Justin started taking the Paxil, and it did help control his symptoms more, but the side effects were something Justin didn't handle very well. It killed his sex drive, which was fine with me since I had a hysterectomy earlier in the year. Even at that, it was hard to imagine being 27 and 31 and facing the possibility our sex life was pretty much over. I knew Justin wasn't happy when he started to talk about if we could possibly do other types of therapy instead of taking all these medications with the nasty side effects. When we discussed this at the therapy appointments, I quickly realized the VA didn't offer much of anything else for treatment of PTSD. Their approach seemed to be: Treat the symptoms, not the *cause* of the symptoms, which meant just keep shoving pills down Justin's throat.

I felt like the VA really didn't care that much about Justin, but I never shared that feeling with him. They just wanted him to take his pills, shut up, be a good boy, and then go away. When we would discuss our lack of sex with the VA, they were more content with trying to get us to accept that our sex life was over. *Hell no, we weren't going to accept that! There had to be a better way!*

We continued to go to therapy trying our best to figure everything out until March 2010. While I was finishing up my letter that would go along with Justin's stressor letter, we got a denial letter for his disability claim. I didn't understand it; we had until August to get everything turned in. We called the regional office to find out what was going on. We were told, just like it said in the denial letter, that Justin's claim was denied because of lack of proof that the stressor occurred during his military service. They acknowledged that he had been receiving treatment at the Vet Center and at the VA for PTSD, but without additional evidence, they couldn't find that it was service connected. We explained that we thought we had one year from the date of file to submit additional evidence, and they just kept saying that was true. Our next question was, "So if we send you these letters and news clips, the claim will be continued like this denial letter never existed, right?" Their response was that we had one year from the date of the denial letter to submit additional evidence or file an appeal. Alright, that *still* didn't answer our question, so we asked again if our case would be picked up right where it left off. They gave us the same answer as before. Talking to them was like talking to a brick wall! Out of frustration I asked the lady, "You're not going to go away from your scripted answer, are you?" She responded by telling me that she had already answered my question and was sorry it wasn't what I wanted to hear. We were getting nowhere so I told her I would find the answers elsewhere and hung up. Justin looked at me and said, "They don't care at all."

I couldn't help but agree. It felt like being on trial only in reverse. We're the victims here, but we have the burden of proof. In our case, we had some news footage of the plane crash of the arrested landing that went wrong and a newspaper article talking about the accident that mentioned Justin by name as proof that he was there and that it was a traumatic event, but they didn't consider it credible evidence because it wasn't coming straight from the military.

Justin

When Shawn started working on the stressor letter, I didn't understand why she needed so much help. She kept asking me how I felt when things were happening. I couldn't answer that; I didn't want to think about it. She should've had enough in her journal from all the counseling sessions. She always took notes and then put it all in her journal. I just couldn't do it, and I knew she could. I wanted so badly to get back to normal, not keep reliving everything that happened.

Every time something would happen the VA's answer was to give me another pill with more side effects. I didn't want to spend the rest of my life doped up and barely able to live. Once they denied my claim I thought, *That's it. No more. No one gives a shit.* I stopped going to therapy and thought Shawn and I would figure everything out on our own. I mean, we were doing much better now; I was doing much better. I knew we would be able to deal with anything that came our way.

HOME

October 2009 — June 2010

Shawn

With Justin's past work history and now his disability claim being denied, I was concerned about how we would make ends meet. Fortunately after our Xbox 360 repair business came to a halt in October 2009, I had started looking for other ways to make money from home. I had done some research and realized people were making a lot of money by selling information products online. So after doing some digging, I decided to write an Xbox 360 DVD repair guide. There were no other guides like this, and we thought we'd hit the jackpot! I spent the next two months writing a how-to repair guide. But I quickly found out that writing a book and putting it up for sale weren't enough. There was so much more involved when it came to marketing that I didn't know beforehand. Over the next few months I learned everything I could about working online and through trial and error became very good at getting Web traffic where I wanted it. By March 2010, I'd started teaching people how to work from home using social media marketing, so we had some money coming into the house.

Justin was impossible after being denied by the VA. All he did was sit and watch TV. The kids ran wild, Justin didn't do anything at all, and I was left to figure everything out. He wouldn't go to therapy at all nor go to the VA appointments for his medicine. He didn't have a job and wasn't looking for one at all. I didn't know what to do.

We started fighting a lot again because I was spending so much time on the computer trying to build up our book sales. Every time we'd fight, he would tell me how I didn't do anything. One night we got into a really bad fight about money and getting rid of some of our animals. At that point we had two pit bulls and two cats. Our finances were tight, and we didn't have the money to keep feeding them all. Plus, we couldn't get rid of the fleas. Justin took off in a rage driving like a bat out of hell. He ended up clipping a guy who was walking down the highway with his truck mirror. He didn't realize he had hit a person. He did stop to see what he had hit, but he didn't see anything so he came back home.

I ended up calling 911 and explaining to them what had happened. I said if anyone called in saying that they got hit that it was us. Justin was furious that I called, but all I could think was, *Hit and run.* Later that night the Sheriff called us back and let us know we needed to come down to the station. When we got there, they explained that Justin had in fact hit someone, and the man was being taken to the hospital to receive stitches in his arm. They filled out the police report, and then because he hit a pedestrian, Justin's license would be suspended for 6 months. All I could think about was, *Without therapy, we're heading back to the way things were before.*

Justin

When Shawn had the idea for this book, I thought, *Awesome! This will make us money, and we can sit back and let it run on autopilot.* But that didn't happen. I knew it couldn't be that easy. Shawn spent all day everyday on the computer working, but she didn't get paid for all the hours she spent doing it. I had to take care of the kids all the time. Cooking, laundry, bedtimes... You name it; I did it. I was getting very sick of having to do it all. She did nothing but turn and tell me at least she was bringing in money. What the hell is happening? This isn't what it was supposed to be like! But the fighting continued, and I had no choice but to start leaving the house to blow off some steam.

I would always just go for a drive and turn up my music. The night I hit that guy, I was on my way back home and had calmed down. It was dark, and the guy was wearing black walking in the turn lane. It wasn't my fault, but I still turned around to see if I would see something, but I didn't see anything. I was so mad at Shawn for calling 911. I got even madder when we went down to the station and they asked me what model of Dodge I was driving. Are you kidding me? They never would have figured out it was me! I was driving a Chevy S-10 extreme. There is no Dodge that looks like my vehicle. And they thought it was black, not midnight blue. When we got back home, I couldn't help myself. I told Shawn it was her fault I was losing my driver's license.

Shawn

I couldn't do this again, so I had to figure out how to gain control fast. I remembered what his first therapist told me. "Justin has to learn there are consequences for his actions." Even though he wasn't out of control like he had been a year ago, the longer he was without his medicine, the worse it was getting. So I felt her advice still applied here. I told him to either start looking for a job or start doing something around the house and gave him a week to figure out what he was going to do.

During that time, I refused to do anything around the house at all; I just kept focusing on our internet business. I didn't do the dishes or any laundry. If the kids made a mess, it just stayed. I figured at some point he wouldn't be able to take it anymore and would get up and do something. But he never did. I didn't know how to help him through this state, but once again I came back to the idea of him taking consequences for actions. So I got the kids together, and told Justin that we were going to stay in the camper and that I wouldn't come back in the house until it was cleaned up. I don't know if he understood how serious I was. I thought that would get his butt in gear. I wasn't going to harp on him; he knew my terms and that was it. I was not going to budge on this decision. And he was going to have to deal with me working all the time since he wasn't interested in finding a job. Problem was, my idea backfired. He stayed in the camper with us and was very content staying there. We stayed camping for weeks, and I wondered if he was just going to have us stay living there forever.

We ran back to the house, and I dropped Justin over at his brother's to help him work on his car. When I finished grabbing what I needed at the house, I checked the mail and sat in the truck looking through it. While I was sitting there, a sheriff pulled up right in front of me. I got out of the truck and asked him if he needed something. He explained that they had received a call about the welfare of our animals. He said he had checked on the dogs in the back yard and that they seemed to be okay, but when he came to knock on the door, one of our cats was in the window and looked very sick. He said he could also see in the front room and could tell there were clothes everywhere. I explained that, yes, the house was a bit of a mess but that right then the kids and I weren't living there. I told him that I was trying to teach Justin a lesson and that he had to get it cleaned back up before we would come back. He explained that he needed to get into the house and check it out. I told him I didn't have the key and that we would have to wait for Justin.

When Justin got there, the sheriff started talking to him, and Justin told him the house key was in the camper. At that point I asked if he had a warrant, and the sheriff quickly reminded Justin that his license was suspended and he was just driving, so we could, "Do this the easy way or the hard way." Justin immediately got in the truck, got the keys, and took the sheriff to the house. Another sheriff had pulled up and asked to speak to me. He wanted to know what was going on in our house. He started asking me about our history: The domestic disturbance call, Justin hitting a pedestrian, the calls to Child Protective Services, and what all the repaired holes in the wall were about. I explained to him that Justin had PTSD and had been receiving help at the Vet Center and the VA. But as far as the calls to CPS, they found nothing to be wrong and that the kids were happy and well taken care of. The only reason they'd been called out was because Justin was mowing the lawn one day, Jesse got loose and ran over to a neighbor's house, and the neighbor decided to turn us in.

When they were finished, they ended up charging us both with animal neglect, but didn't arrest us. As soon as we left, I was on the phone with the Vet Center and explained to Justin's counselor what was going on. We talked about him not coming in for the last three months and him being denied for his disability claim. She told me to get him in there and that she would also get him an appointment with his VA doctor so we could get the meds going again. She told me to tell him it would look better in court if he was attending counseling sessions. And that is exactly what I told Justin to get him back into therapy.

Justin

Okay, so maybe I should have taken what Shawn said more seriously, but I just wasn't dealing with doing everything at the house all the time. It was like she was addicted to the computer and didn't want to do anything with the family any longer. When she said her and the kids were going to stay in the camper, I thought, *Great! We can focus on being a family now and get things headed in the right direction.* I was happy spending time as a family, and I didn't want to leave them. I felt like I was losing Shawn when she started working online, but now we were back together again—safe.

I wasn't expecting the cops to show up at the house. When Shawn was with the cops, I didn't understand why she didn't just say she didn't know where I was at. Once I got down there, they had me on driving on a suspended license if I didn't let them in the house. So I had no choice but to let them in. When we went in, they walked around the house, and they just told me to get the dishes done, clean up the clothes in the front room, and pick up all the kids toys. But they checked out the cat, and she did look very sick. She was starting to lose her hair on her back and tail. They asked if we had taken the cat to the vet, and I explained that with me not working, money was tight. It wasn't something we could afford right now. Plus, the cat was 8 years old. Since we hadn't taken her to a veterinarian, they got us on animal neglect. Shawn was furious.

We were back at the house the next day cleaning it up, and it took a couple of days to get the job done. The cops had threatened to come back and check up on us, but they never showed up.

We could have moved back in right away, but Shawn insisted I go back to therapy before she'd let that happen. When she told me about going back to the VA and Vet Center, I knew she was right: I had to go. As much as I hated it, I was out of control when I wasn't on any medicine or going to therapy. So I agreed to go back and stick with it this time. Once I got back in and got my meds again, it took about two weeks before I started noticing a difference. During that time, we talked a lot in therapy about what got me so aggravated during the last few months. I told her when my claim was denied, I felt like my time in service didn't amount to anything. I mean I came home and couldn't find a job. I wanted to become a police officer, and that couldn't happen because I got screwed up in the Navy. And then I was denied help for being screwed up because they couldn't find that my PTSD was service connected. I was on my own! I had been out of work for a year then and no idea where to even look for a job. I wasn't used to having to take care of the kids and everything else all the effin' time. All Shawn did was work on the computer. She didn't talk, didn't do anything with me or the kids, and just didn't seem to care anymore. So that was why I started getting so mad. I just couldn't handle things anymore. I screwed up. If I would have stayed on my meds, none of this would have happened.

She then asked me why Shawn's working bothered me. I told her that Shawn working wasn't so much the issue; it was how much she was working. Shawn would work 16 hours every single day. And she is one of these people that when she is doing something, she gets so focused that she doesn't notice anything else around her going on. I just didn't understand what she had to do that took that much time. At least when we were repairing the Xbox 360 consoles, we were making very good money for the hours we put in.

Shawn

Sitting there listening to Justin talk to the counselor, I felt like he was having a big ol' pity party. I tried to explain to Justin that just because we wrote the book and put it up for sale, didn't mean it would magically sell itself. We had to market it, which takes time. He turned and asked why I didn't put it up on eBay or post in some gamer forums that we have this repair book for sale. I could tell he really didn't get how much work I was doing. More than that, I felt like he expected me to do everything! I didn't care anymore about making him understand. But as a last ditch effort I was going to explain it all to the counselor so that she could make him understand it. I was all out of patience and sick and tired of trying. I didn't think he had any right to be questioning me. I was done being the sole bread-winner while he was just sitting on his ass. I was just done.

I fell back on my old ways of debate team from high school and listed my evidence points one at a time.

I said, "First of all, I can't put it up on eBay because it's not a physical property that gets shipped out. Next, I have to publish good quality articles so that people will start to see me as an expert. Once they realize I'm an expert, then they start trusting what I say, and then they will buy the book. Right now, I'm trying to figure out how Google ranks us in the search results. At this moment, they don't even know we exist. So if someone searches for an Xbox 360 repair guide, we don't even show up yet. I know I have to create good backlinks to make us show up on the first page, but the formula isn't exact. Plus for every backlink, I have to have a totally new article, and it might take hundreds of them for Google to notice! And I can't just go around posting the book everywhere; that's spamming, which could not only knock us down in Google, but could also take away what credibility I've built."

Both Justin and the therapist looked at me like I was speaking in Greek. Justin asked me if I was sure I knew what I was doing. I thought he was stupid for asking me that. I sarcastically told him, "Well, yeah! I must be doing something right. For some reason, through my writing I'm catching people's attention and actually helping them! They seem to enjoy my personal stories of what I'm learning and want to hear more about the how I'm directing online traffic to boost attention to my book."

I wouldn't have had that kind of attention if I was just wasting my time. I knew I was on to something good, and Justin wasn't getting how important it was, nor was he attempting to help me in any way. I was getting more positive attention from the people on the Internet than I was from him.

Justin of course had to throw in his two cents. “No one else working online has to do all this. And they definitely don’t work for free teaching people what they’re learning. That’s nuts! And explain to me how any of this that you’re doing is benefiting our family, because it has nothing to do with the Xbox book.”

I looked at the counselor and told her, “See? This is how he talks to me. If he ain’t yelling, he’s putting me down. Everything I do is stupid!”

Of course Justin didn’t think he was doing anything wrong. His reply was, “Well they don’t! No one would work all those hours for very little sales. And they’re smart enough to not work for free! And they keep their eye on the ball.”

I was so mad at him right then that I couldn’t control my mouth, nor did I want to! I wasn’t screeching, but through my tone I was one pissed off, cold bitch. “You haven’t worked for a year. You haven’t attempted to find a job, but yet I’m the one trying anything and everything to keep money coming in, and you’re gonna sit there and dog me? At least I’m doing something.”

Justin quickly snapped back, “Well I would, but I’ve been waiting on you!”

“Why don’t you get up off your lazy ass and do something?!? You’re grown! Damn, you’re as bad as a kid. Waiting on me? More like waiting for me to do it for you!” I said as I stormed out of the office.

I sat out in the hallway for a few moments fighting back the tears. I felt like Justin was a third child because he couldn't make decisions without me. But if I made decisions for him, then he got mad because he felt like I was making him out to be less of a man. It was like he thought I enjoyed things this way, but nothing could be further from the truth. When I got married, I had wanted a man who was capable of doing what needed to be done for the family. Instead I had someone who was dependent on me for most everything and mad at me for it. He had no initiative. At that point, he could have done the wrong thing, but I would have preferred that because it would have been something. Once again he couldn't let go of that military life, and he had turned into someone who had to be told to do everything. It was like he couldn't think separate from me; I had to think for him but not let him know that I was doing it. I didn't want to give my husband orders when he was supposed to be my equal.

After a bit in the hall, I calmed down. Somewhere inside I knew this was just part of the whole PTSD situation we had to work on. I remembered *Full Metal Jacket* and how those guys had been trained to follow orders just like Justin had. I knew I wouldn't quit entirely, despite storming out of the office. I had walked out on the situation, but I didn't walk out on him. Like a boxer in the ring, I knew I had to go back inside for another round.

When I walked back into the counselor's office she asked if I was alright. I told her yeah, I'd be fine. I tried to tell her that I was sorry, but she brushed it off.

She started talking to us about our communication skills. We were told to start making "I" statements instead of using "You." The counselor felt that would help a lot. And she also wanted us to write down how things were going with it: Did it still escalate? Were we able to remain calm and talk? Things like that. Then we were to bring our responses back with us the following week. As we were leaving she handed me some papers to be filled out to send to the VA so Justin's disability case could be re-opened.

Later that week Justin got a job, so I was very relieved. Not that I didn't enjoy spending time with Justin, but we seemed to get along a lot better when we got some time apart. He told me to quit working online, but I knew Justin's track record with jobs. Working online was my backup plan, the only chance I had of bringing in money if his employment fell through.

I was trying to figure out which direction I wanted the online business to go. I had the Xbox book, but I was pretty good at social media marketing and teaching others how to work from home. Problem was, there were so many people doing that it would be hard to make money. I needed to find my niche. So I decided to let it go for a bit and get working on Justin's PTSD claim paperwork. The next part I tackled was the spouse's letter I still needed to finish. It was only a couple of weeks later that I had a finished version.

Meanwhile, Justin and I were working really hard to follow the counselor's advice about using "I" statements instead of "you" statements, which was actually helping us a lot! We also tried to do a lot of things together as a family, such as going camping. We continued to go to counseling, and Justin continued to work. All of this was bringing us closer together, and I could feel us getting more comfortable with each other. For the first time in a long time, I really felt like our house was a home.

PURPOSE

June 2010 — April 2011

Shawn

While doing research online, I had the hardest time finding any information for spouses of vets. I looked and looked, but there was very little information about dealing with a husband who has PTSD. And what information I could find didn't seem to tell it like it really was. *How are spouses supposed to know how to live with this? How are they going to know what's normal and not normal?* It hit me then: all those spouses that were getting ready for their troops to come home were in no better position than I was when Justin first came home. Nothing had changed. I took out my letter I had written for Justin's disability claim and started looking it over.

Justin and I met when he was 6 and I was 10. He played on my brother's basketball team, and then I became his babysitter. So Justin and I have known each other since we were kids, and we stayed in contact until I went to high school. We didn't resume contact until Justin was already in the Navy. Justin came home for Christmas break December of 2001, and while shopping with his brothers for Christmas gifts, he came to T.G.I. Friday's where I was a waitress. It was funny to see Justin all grown up, but it didn't take me long to realize that it was the same old Justin. From that point on we were inseparable.

We talked every chance we got, we e-mailed, and he would come home whenever he could swing a few days off. Justin was great with my daughter, he treated me with the utmost respect, and he was just a fun guy to be around.

In June 2002, the USS George Washington was deployed to support Operation Enduring Freedom in the Middle East and Arabian Gulf. Right before deployment Justin was assigned to the military police. Justin thought he'd finally found his home. He really enjoyed his position and excelled at being a military police officer.

Justin would e-mail me every chance he got, but for the most part we had to resort to snail mail. Our relationship continued growing it and it wasn't long before we were discussing our future plans together. Justin came home for Valentine's Day in 2003, and of course, that's when he proposed to me. There was nothing that could bring us down that week. We started planning our wedding which was going to be in September 2003. When it was time for him to leave, we decided that I would take a vacation in March and come visit him in Norfolk, Virginia.

In March 2003, Justin had to attend an anti-terrorism training course for one week where he learned different types of terrorist tactics, ran mock terrorist drills, and was certified on many different weapons.

I arrived in Virginia right after this training course was completed. Justin told me that our September wedding was not possible because they were unsure when they were going to be deployed again. This left us only two options: elope or wait until Justin was out of the military. So of course we eloped.

Justin returned home June 29, 2004. I was so excited to have him home. Our baby was due within the next two weeks, and I was ready to settle down into married life. Little did I know this was the beginning of what would be a five year nightmare. I expected it to take a little time for Justin to get used to not being in the military and to readjust to civilian life. I mean he went from someone telling him what to do and where to be, to having a wife, a stepdaughter, and a baby due any time. I guess the first thing I noticed was that any form of intimacy was nonexistent. Just holding hands or giving me a kiss almost always would turn into a fight. I was left feeling very alone and confused. We had not seen each other in 6 months, and he was not interested at all in having sex.

A week after his return home our daughter was born. I remember his face, and for a brief few days thought I had my husband back. He was such a proud dad and a very good father. But that, too, would disappear very quickly.

Once we were back home and getting settled in, I started to unpack Justin's bags. He flipped out. I didn't understand what was going on and kept telling him that this was his home and he didn't have to live out of his bag any more. It would be two months before I was able to fully unpack his bags.

Justin started having nightmares shortly after our daughter was born. He would start yelling in his sleep and kicking and hitting things. I made the mistake one night of grabbing his arm trying to wake him up. He raised his head up, pointed to his arm, and said, "You see this? I will kill you with it." Well needless to say, that completely freaked me out. I could barely sleep the rest of the night.

During of one of our fights, I told Justin I didn't care

about all the nice things we had. I told him I would rather live in a shack if it meant getting my husband back. That obviously didn't sit very well with him. He flew off the handle calling me ungrateful and any other name you can think of. Normally at this point, I would go off by myself and cry and let him go to avoid a bigger conflict, but for some reason I decided to open my mouth. I told him that he was materialistic and that his toys meant more to him than his family.

The next thing I knew, he went back to our bedroom, got his gun, and brought it right back into the room that I was in. I took a step back not sure what he was going to do. I know he saw the horror on my face, but I had pushed him too far. He got right in my face, cocked the gun, and started waving it around yelling at me "What do you want me to shoot? I'll take it all out myself. There will be nothing left. I will shoot this whole fucking house up." I was terrified. I fell back on the couch not sure whether to look him in the eye or not. All the while thinking, "This is it. I'm going to die." I let him yell and scream, and I didn't say word. I didn't know if I might say something that would set him off and make him start shooting.

He stayed in his rage for what seemed like forever, until finally he put the gun down, looked at me, said, "Do what you want," and walked out the door to go work. I sat there after he left trying to figure out what just happened. I had never seen him so angry. It was like he snapped and had no control over his actions.

When I finally pulled myself together, I called the VA hospital to try to get him in to see someone. This has gone on years and years. His nightmares have slowed down some, but now he gets angry easily, he still doesn't trust people, and he comes off cold and distant. He used to be gentle; now he shows no emotions. He used to be supportive; now he acts like he doesn't care.

Shawn J. Gourley

Reading over the letter, I started to wonder if I couldn't share my story about living with PTSD as a way of helping other spouses understand the situation the same way my stories about Xbox machine repair were helping people learn about that. I wasn't thinking of making money off people's pain. In my heart, I just wanted to help them get informed. More than that, I thought my situation with Justin and my writing ability put me in a position where I could really help people know what could actually happen if PTSD goes untreated so they could get help quicker. I never wanted anyone else to go through the hell I had. I also thought it would be another way to get my name out there as a work-from-home expert because many spouses living with people who have PTSD are forced to work-from-home, just like I had been. As much as I wanted to help them, I was also hoping to keep money coming into our house so that we could stay afloat. It was a fine line to walk between making money off PTSD and trying to keep my other job going, so I decided I would write and give away a free book about my PTSD experiences to make absolutely certain that I wasn't crossing that line.

Giving the book away as a digital download was the only way I knew to provide it free to the masses without spending a lot of extra money to print copies to give away. And besides that, a download would be instant, and I wouldn't have the same hassles with shipping stuff out as I did with the Xbox machines that I repaired.

I took Justin's PTSD stressor letter and my letter and combined them into one to make up the contents of the free book. In July 2010 I started making a Facebook Fan page and named it Military with PTSD™. I really didn't know what to expect when I started the page. I thought maybe I'd find more women like me who were tired of fighting with their vets and tired of fighting the VA to get help. But I suspected that there would be a lot of anger, so I thought I had better set things up right to take care of it. I laid out some very specific ground rules for this page. Firstly and most importantly, this was a place to give away my free book. Secondly, I wanted to help spouses prepare for when their members of the armed forces came home and give them an understanding of what could really happen, so there would be no selling or solicitations of any kind on the page. Thirdly, the page would be open so spouses could talk and get support from one another. Lastly, as rule for myself, I wasn't going to hide the side of me who was an Internet marketer, just to make sure people didn't think I was trying to sneak my way into selling them something. I thought I had all the ground work laid out, but very quickly everything started changing.

Justin

When Shawn started talking about making a book to help spouses deal with PTSD, I didn't know what to think. I couldn't understand how anything she was doing would help us make money online. And I definitely didn't get how anything would be accomplished by giving it away for free. But I had a job at this point so I wasn't too worried. I just let her do what she thought she needed to do.

I think partly I didn't connect what she was doing with anything that was going on in my life. I got the idea that I was treating her like crap and needed to improve, but I don't think I'd fully accepted PTSD in the rest of my life yet. For her to be writing a book about dealing with it didn't seem connected to our life in any real way. I just tried to go to therapy, go to work, and not try to get into too many fights with her.

Shawn

In August 2010, I had the Facebook page up and running. The book wasn't finished yet, but I knew it would be very shortly. I let the members of the page decide on the title of the book and tell me exactly what they wanted to know. For a change I had work I really believed in, and when I wasn't busy with the book and the page, I was camping with the family and just trying to keep life going smoothly. Mostly, Justin and I stayed out of each other's way and did our own thing.

Everything was going great until Justin got fired, but he was only mad for about a day. It was only a couple of more days until he had another job. Sadly, that one only lasted a week before he got fired again. Both times he was fired because people didn't like working with him. He was too meticulous and too quick to point out other people's mistakes to his bosses. He was even too quick to point out his bosses' mistakes! This was the exact same kind of thinking that had got him suspended for taking off half a day with only leaving a note just like his boss did all the time. To him, bosses and employees should be held to the same standards. Again, that was the way things were run in the military, and again his PTSD made it hard for him to let go of that thinking because the military way had kept him alive. I still didn't like him getting fired all the time, but at least I understood it better and didn't get so angry about it. I also didn't panic because I knew that the work I was doing was hopefully going to take that burden off of him.

By the end of August 2010, our focus in the home was all about getting the kids back into the swing of school. Jaxson started preschool for the first time, and Jesse was in first grade. With the kids out of the house part of the day, Justin started to turn some attention to me and even started to get involved with what I was doing online. The return to routine seemed to be good for all of us and a kind of peace settled on us.

I came to appreciate our new-found peace even more when I saw all the stuff people talked about on our Facebook page. Very quickly we had attracted thousands of members, and not just spouses. The vets themselves were coming on the page and starting to talk about things that no one else seemed to understand. When President Obama announced that we would be pulling out of Iraq and that the "war was over," the vets started talking about how they wished they could split open their heads and show Obama the insides because for them, the war was far from over. Some of them sounded just like Justin as they talked about employers who didn't understand them and wives who just didn't get it. I saw that domestic violence and suicide attempts were more the norm than the exception. I also saw that emotional abuse was pretty standard, and so many of the spouses were going through the same types of things that Justin and I had just gotten out of. But the main thing I saw was that there seemed to be this feeling of "us" vs. "them" when it came to the rest of the world who knew nothing about PTSD. It got me to thinking about the vets I had known in the past.

My grandfather was a WWII veteran who had PTSD pretty bad, but they called it "shell shock" back then, and no one knew what that meant. To us, he was a drunk who always left his family without food because he'd rather go drink his money away. We knew that he'd seen his best friend's head cut off by an airplane propeller, but we couldn't connect that up with how *mean* he was. He got the kind of medical help he needed from the VA, but it wasn't for PTSD. But despite all that, I still respected him for giving his service to our country, even if others didn't, and I knew a lot of other people also respected WWI and WWII vets. But the vets I saw in my parents' generation who came back from Vietnam went through a lot of anger and hatred directed at them because a lot of Americans didn't think they belonged over there, like the vets had any choice but to do what the government told them to do after they'd been drafted. And that attitude seemed a little closer to what I was seeing for the vets that were coming back from the Middle East. A lot of people didn't believe in what was going on over there, but also there was this idea that anytime something like a suicide or violent outburst happened, people would say stuff like, "Oh, it's probably just another crazy vet going off! We'd better lock 'em all up so we'll be safe." Few people outside of the military lifestyle seemed to know, care, or understand how big of a problem PTSD was and how much it was affecting the lives of military families. My eyes were being opened.

Being able to talk about these things on the page seemed to help the vets and their families, so we made it very clear that they should be allowed to talk about whatever they wanted as long as it related to PTSD. These vets had fought hard for their freedom of speech, so as long as they weren't being hateful or making personal attacks, any opinion was okay. That seemed to make the page even more popular. It continued to grow and was starting to attract some attention and landed me a few interviews with blogs, radio, and television. But in a way, all that attention was making me nervous.

Justin

In September 2010, Shawn started freaking out over the book she was writing. We both had started to see that she was on to something and getting more attention that she had ever planned on. But she started saying stuff about how she couldn't release the book to the world because she thought it portrayed me as a monster. She was bawling her eyes out and ready to delete the whole thing. She kept saying, "I can't do this! I can't do this to you!" I stopped her from backing out by telling her, "It is what it is. I can't change what I did." I knew some people would be mad at me for what happened, but I also knew that the book was important to Shawn and might be important to other people. So I told her she had to keep going.

However, as much as I wanted to see her keep going with this and didn't mind that our story would be out there, I still didn't like going on the Facebook page. I knew the people there didn't understand why I had done what I did, and I didn't think they liked me. I also just didn't like talking to people very much, especially in large groups. As the page grew, it started to look like a big crowd to me, so I left all that part of it to Shawn.

Shawn

In October we finally released the mini-book as a free download. The response was overwhelming. I was getting emails from spouses and parents thanking me daily for the book and the Facebook page. They were telling me how nice it was to know they weren't alone. Spouses were saying that my book had saved their marriage. But it took getting one special email to help me realize this book was not just helping spouses; it was helping veterans. It wasn't the best-written email I'd ever read, but it was clearly written from the heart, and I have cried over it many times.

> "the book opened my mind up to things that i did not know that was the same thing going on with me right now and i thought it was just me now i know its not just me its the way things are for ppl like me yes its not well in the norm for ppl but its more norm for ppl like us i have a bud thats in and he told me about the site and he is apart of it so i went and looked and wow it has opened my eyes i thought i was just a loser that did not make

> the cut after i did what i needed to do but i see its not that im a loser all f up its i just .... well still getting to that point . this Book is good in a way that it dose not hide or mask the bs that ppl deal with. my now ex i had her read it and she just could not understand why it was made. its one of the well you had to be there to know kinds of things if everyone just would take 10 min and know wow i dont act the way i did before I went in and i know that I just wish that 1/2 the ppl would know what any vet and on duty ppl do for them it would be a difrint world. this book has open my eyes to know im not a f up person that hates himself and everyone but that i do just need some help and i am woking on that now that i see that im not just a bad man im just who i am now."

Some days I had to read this email again to let me know that what I was doing was making a difference and to keep me going when dealing with all of this got overwhelming. There started to be more posts daily and more emails. I didn't know how to react to everything, but we were quickly becoming a huge online support group for people living with PTSD, and that included us as well. It was really nice to hear others talking so openly about how PTSD is such an "invisible" disability. It's not like being in a wheelchair or having some body deformity that can visually let someone else know the vets have something going on inside. People with PTSD look just like everyone else, but they do not think, speak, or act like people would normally expect them to. Some people on the page even suggested wearing a PTSD medical bracelet to let others know they have the condition, but other people on the page thought that would put them at a disadvantage on high functioning days. There just didn't seem to be a good answer to this one, except to raise awareness on the topic, which is what I hoped my page would start to do.

I also started to see that a lot of what I thought were just weird little quirks about Justin were actually things that happened to a lot of vets with PTSD, like the thing about Justin not wanting to answer the phone. There started to be a lot of discussions on the page about how freakin' vague the DSM is when it comes to describing symptoms of PTSD. The page was helping all of us see the specifics of how behavior all fit the patterns described by the VA.

We also started seeing patterns of how the VA was treating us. The nightmare with all the paperwork seemed to be everyone's story! Getting a vet diagnosed with PTSD seemed to require a freakin' act of God! And not only that, but everyone was talking about how the VA loses paperwork all the time. Add on top of that the little dance with the VA doctors when it came to filing a claim. First of all, to even be diagnosed with PTSD so the VA will recognize it, they require vets to only see VA doctors. And then if vets still wanted to file a claim, rather than just keeping shoving pills down their throats, they had to go get a second evaluation from *another* VA doctor to get the claim pushed through! It seemed like they were just looking for a way to write vets off as having "adjustment disorder," rather than saying it was PTSD. Many of the people on the page started instructing vets who were going in for evaluation to not talk about their childhoods so that the VA wouldn't have any fodder to say that their current condition was based on something from before they went into the military. But the absolute worst of it was that the VA does *nothing* for spouses and other family members who are catching the brunt of the vet's behavior and even getting Secondary PTSD.

Some days the level of the frustration with the VA on the page was high enough that it could not be measured using existing technology. It didn't take me long at all to realize that a big part of why the VA was getting away with how they were treating vets with PTSD was because no one had been talking about the problems all in one place. On the Facebook page, we were suddenly able to see into each other's lives and see what was going on behind closed doors. Something else I could suddenly see was that the VA wasn't singling me out. They weren't *listening* to any of the spouses or any other family member, just like all the times I tried calling for help before they would actually see us.

The members of the Facebook page could see the benefit of all our discussions and my disclosures in the free mini-book as well because they started requesting that I put the book in print at this time. I explained to them that a print book would be something they would have to buy because it costs money to put things in print, but they said they wanted it anyhow. I couldn't understand why they would want to pay for something that they could get for free, but they kept insisting they wanted to have an actual book they could hold in their hands, even though this was something I couldn't provide for free. I finally agreed and decided that I would add more content to the book because if they were going to pay for it, I wanted to make sure they were getting good value for the price.

I asked the Facebook page readers what they wanted in the book, and they gave me a list of things: They wanted to know more about our therapy, they wanted to know more of my emotions, but most of all they wanted to know Justin's side of everything. That last one was going to be a difficult task in and of itself, but I set out to work on it a little bit every day. I asked Justin questions about how he felt and what he was thinking in response to everything I was writing. Even as we started the process I knew this would take me months to accomplish.

But I also quickly realized how important of a process it was. We shared some of our conversations on the Facebook Page and learned even more from the other members. I remember how surprised I was when I posted the note on Justin's porn addiction. What I had thought was just a problem in our relationship turned out to be a problem for a lot of vets. I also became extra-grateful for all my note-taking in counseling. Whenever Justin didn't have a lot to say on a topic, I could look at my old notes to find ways to fill the gaps.

In December 2010, Justin got a new job as a machinist. We knew it was only a temp job because he was working to replace someone who was on strike with the rest of the Union workers. At first this job seemed to be good for him because it was the kind of work he was best at. Not only was it the best suited job for his skills, it was a job where he was told what to do all the time and didn't have to make his own decisions. But the job quickly turned more difficult as they started making him work twelve-hour shifts, moving around his day and night schedule, and not giving him enough down time between shifts to rest.

By that time, the stuff I was doing online put me in contact with a lot of folks who were dealing with PTSD. Justin was really involved in my work, and those people helped him to better cope with all these changes at work because they understood his thinking better than even I did.

Justin

After Shawn released the book, a few people on the Facebook page started asking me questions about what I was thinking during certain events Shawn described. I started trying to answer as best I could, but sometimes what I said got people mad. Some veterans said I wasn't a real combat vet because I hadn't been involved in actual fighting. But when one guy started trying to make Shawn out to be nothing more than a slick Internet marketer, I got real mad and started going off on him. I think people could see how protective I was of Shawn after that, and they started to like me more and ask me even more questions. And soon after that, we cleared up with the page that I was a combat vet because I had served in a combat zone in support of OEF and OIF. Slowly but surely, I started to be accepted by the group.

When they started asking Shawn to put the book into print and include my side of it, I wasn't sure I wanted to do that. But I could see how it might help people understand what goes on inside the mind of a person with PTSD, so I decided to help Shawn out. I didn't feel like I had a lot to say, but she helped by asking me a lot of questions. I did my best to answer them, even though sometimes I wasn't sure of what she was getting at. She wanted me to expand on my answers when I felt I'd already said all I needed to say. How many ways are there to say, "I was mad," or "I didn't like it," anyhow? I found myself saying, "I don't know," a lot. I also told her, "You've got it all written down in your journal from the counseling sessions. Just go find it!"

Shawn

Then in January 2011 disaster struck. I started passing kidney stones that not only brought my work on the book to a screeching halt, but forced Justin to be the front runner on the page. That was so far out of his comfort zone!!! But it starting helping him in more ways than I could ever imagine.

It all started one night when a mother asked Justin why her son who was in the hospital was freaking out every time she would try to touch him. He responded by saying, "He's not freaking out because of you, it's a defense reaction. You gotta think, when we're on duty and overseas our training to be alert is what keeps us alive. We don't even let our crew members come up behind us. Think about it: If the enemy was able to get close enough to you to grab your weapon, you're dead. So no matter who it is, we're always on alert to protect ourselves. You trust no one, and that is how you survive. That is trained into us from day one. It's not something you can just turn off because you're home. It's gonna take him some time to feel safe again." That mother got it then, along with a bunch of the spouses on the page. And they were hungry for more—much more information from Justin and the other veterans on the page. At that point Justin and I understood exactly what the page wanted. So we started taking parts of the book along with what Justin was saying and laying it out on the Facebook page in the notes section so they could give us feedback.

They loved the back and forth dialogue we were doing between the two of us and asked if we could keep it that way in the book. We agreed and changed the entire layout of the book so that throughout each section they were getting both sides of the story from both views. The book had quickly gone from 28 pages to 150 pages! I was happy with it and started looking for an editor. I also started sending the manuscript to agents at that time to see if it would get picked up by anyone. During this time I was still having trouble with my kidneys and started having many surgeries to bust up the stones. Justin had to continue to be the front runner on the page since I was pretty much out of it.

In February 2011, Justin got laid off from work because the strike had ended. It was nice that he hadn't been fired because of his attitude for a change, but it still meant that he had no job. I knew I would have to work extra hard online to bring in some income, but things were looking pretty good for me in that area, so I didn't stress very much. This time though something had drastically changed between Justin and I. We weren't fighting, and for the first time it was very evident we were a strong united couple. Our communication skills had improved very much, and couples were appearing on the page trying to learn and understand what Justin and I had going.

The remainder of February and most of March I spent trying to finish and polish the book that was going into print. I also started getting responses from the agents that I had sent manuscripts to, and sadly not one of them accepted our book. Some gave me some good feedback, but most agents wanted too much changed in the book. I also was getting frustrated with the editors from publishing houses who would actually speak to me. They either wanted me to "tone down" the violent parts of the book, or they said that my writing style didn't, "follow the rules." They also had no clue how important the people on the Facebook page were in creating this book. Not only were those people like family, they had a vested interest in how the book looked when it came out. I especially didn't like it when one editor told me that the people on my page, "didn't know what they wanted." I decided that if by the time the book was completely finished no one was interest in contracting it, then I would go ahead and self-publish.

But then members of the page started trying to help me find ways to publish the book. I was still was in shock that the members of the page were so excited about getting this book into print and that the page membership was growing so rapidly. In just 6 months we had gained over 7,000 followers!

The page members kept telling me that the book was meant to be contracted by a publisher. They were more hopeful than I was, but by this point I was *so* done with agents and editors.

Then one of the page members told me he had a friend who was a writer who might have some ideas on how to market the book. It turned out that she was an editor and publisher. She was able to explain the whole process of publishing a book either as a self-published work or by going through a publisher. She also seemed to really *get* how important the page was to the content of the book and how much they didn't want me to change anything. She also told me that she really liked my writer's Voice and that even though I didn't follow the writing "rules," I was a storyteller with a very important story.

I could hear something in her voice over the phone about how meaningful this book could be. She had PTSD herself, and she said that she thought this book would be very good for all kinds of people, not just military people with PTSD and their families. She could see other people who just wanted to learn more about the subject reading this book and starting to make changes in the way vets with PTSD are treated.

I felt something change in me in that conversation. For the first time, I really felt like I had found my Purpose in life, something that wasn't about how I related to my family or to Justin or to his PTSD. This was something that was for me alone, and it was what had been growing in me for months to help me get through my own situation.

I talked things over with Justin and the Facebook page, and we all thought this publisher really understood what this book was all about, so we decided to contract with them, even though it meant that it would slow down the release of the book by a few months.

In the meantime, I needed to start working on what I was going to say at a benefit concert for incarcerated veterans where I had been invited to speak. There were going to be thousands of people there, and I was the only one scheduled to speak about PTSD.

All of this seemed to bring Justin and me even closer together. When our wedding anniversary rolled around on March 28, he made us chicken nuggets for dinner and sat and watched *Dancing with the Stars* with me. It wasn't a grand gesture of flowers and candy, but it was a small, sweet gift of spending time with me. It helped that I had changed my expectations of him. I had come to value all the peaceful moments with him more than any gift he could buy me. It was just like I always told the people on the page, "Learn to cherish the good times, because when the bad times are there, it makes you look forward to the good times even more." I had stopped fantasizing about "the good old days," or about some rosy future that might never be and had learned to appreciate the man I had right in front of me right now.

Justin's relationship with the page continued to grow. On one of the nights when I was in the hospital for my kidney stones and doped up on painkillers, Justin posted to the page, but he was using my phone so it looked like it was coming from me. When the people started figuring out that it was him, they all had a discussion about me being loopy from the drugs, and Justin told them all that he had shot a video of me singing, "Come Sail Away." They all had a good laugh, and it helped him get through a stressful situation with laughter. It also showed the page how transparent Justin and I are in our communications now since I didn't throw a fit that he'd been using my cell phone. (However, I still can't find the CD of that recording of me singing. He hid it really well!)

On April 30, 2011, I went to Miamisburg, OH, for the veterans benefit concert. Things didn't exactly go as planned. Due to a mix-up, I wasn't able to go on stage, but that turned out to not be a big loss because of all the people that I met there. I met other authors and musicians who were very interested in combining efforts with me to get the word out about veterans with PTSD. In particular I enjoyed meeting authors Boone Cutler and Anthony Farina and musicians SoldierHard TheVoice and Sgt. Leo Dunson. I started to feel like I had allies for my Purpose. I also met with many people who knew of my page already who told me how grateful they were. It was the first time I had gotten the chance to meet any of them face to face, and it was a very emotional day.

One group that impacted me greatly was the families of certain imprisoned soldiers. These soldiers had killed civilians and were incarcerated as murderers. The real tragedy here is that it can be almost impossible to tell the difference between an enemy soldier and a civilian in these wars. There were also family members of vets who had PTSD really bad who were seeing them sent back into combat again and again even though those vets had lost the ability to really tell the difference between right and wrong because of the PTSD.

Some of them were the ones winding up in jail for the rest of their lives because their government had let them down.

I also met vets who were getting DUIs and acting out from PTSD. One guy flipped out bad and rammed a cop car because he thought he was being attacked, and I was handed a pamphlet about a vet who will be in a wheelchair for the rest of his life because the police had to shoot him. There's only just now starting to be a system of intervention for these types of cases called Veterans Court, but it's only a year old and has some problems. Most are set up for DUI and alcohol abuse. There's nothing for cases of domestic abuse. And worst of all, soldiers have to plead guilty to a felony before they can start receiving help.

That day was a real eye-opening experience for me. It added to all I'd been reading on the Facebook page, and showed me I still have so much to learn in certain areas. For example, I don't know much about how to help vets who have traumatic brain injury (TBI) or have endured military sexual trauma (MST) as a cause of their PTSD. And I still don't know if I'm really helping spouses of vets before their vets come home. I remember those books that I was given so long ago before Justin came home. I can see now that they would have been useful to me if I already knew what PTSD was, but the military had given me nothing to describe what to watch for.

What became so clear to me at the concert was that I still have so much work to do in my future. If I had to pick one song to describe how I felt that day, it would be "Carry on my Wayward Son" because carrying on was exactly what I had discovered I need to keep doing until Americans start paying better attention to what's really going on and our vets and their families start getting the help they really need. Carrying on is what all of us affected by PTSD need to keep doing.

Justin

Somehow going through all of this with Shawn helped me to really accept PTSD in myself and that I have a Purpose as well. Just as she is helping the spouses of military with PTSD, I feel like I am helping the vets cope with PTSD. As much as Shawn cares about the vets themselves, she won't ever be able to talk with them like I do. It takes a vet to know a vet, and it takes a vet to talk to a vet. Still, I do feel like Shawn and I are doing this together. She's my battle buddy, and I'm hers.

It's getting easier for me to see the person I used to be and why I did and said the terrible things I did. I try to be honest about that on the Facebook page so that others can learn from my experiences. Once, someone on the page was asking why her boyfriend was acting so abusive to her, threatening suicide and finding other ways of controlling her over the phone, even though he was hundreds of miles away. I said, "Ok, we control because we can. We were taught scare tactics and everything else. We don't trust anyone but our brothers. This is an awful cycle that has to be broken. We control you to stay in control of everything because our lives are out of control. It is abuse. Plain and simple. What I did to Shawn was abuse. I didn't see it that way and neither does your boyfriend right now. But you cannot allow it to continue. You are not responsible or the cause for his actions."

The only thing that makes it easy for me to admit that is because I know that PTSD was the reason behind all that I did. Another time on the Facebook page, I was trying to explain to a spouse who was complaining about her vet's poor behavior that there is usually a good guy deep down under all the bad stuff. I said, "All I keep seeing is posts about how lazy we with PTSD are. You know I was that way not so long ago. I couldn't help it. Between the nightmares and everything else, it was hard to function. It isn't like we can help it." But of course now that I'm on meds, in therapy, and trying to help others, I do have more control over my behavior, and I'm doing my best to get more control every day.

I once said something about the reason behind me getting PTSD on the Facebook page, and I think it might be true. As awful as having PTSD is, I sometimes wonder if the reason I got it at all was so that Shawn and I could be in a position to help others who are going through it. If so, that's a good enough reason for me. I can accept this. I can carry on.

EPILOGUE

Posted on my Facebook profile on May 1, 2011, 9:37 p.m. CST:

President speaking on a matter of National Security in a moment. This late on a Sunday night, can't be good.

Posted on the Military with PTSD Facebook page on May 1, 2011, 10:12 p.m. CST:

This is our day. For everyone that served and the families that stood by while we were deployed. We finally got the SOB. Mission is done. -Justin

Posted on the Military with PTSD Facebook page on May 2, 2011, 12:34 a.m. CST:

Hey everyone! This is Spring Lea Henry, Shawn's editor. We had been tossing around a certain date for releasing her book, and in light of tonight's news, I think it would be a disservice if we didn't go for it. So, we are proud to announce that the release date for War at Home will be September 11, 2011. :)

Posted on the Military with PTSD Facebook page on May 2, 2011, 11:08 a.m. CST:

My turn, remember though I am not a doc or therapist. But I feel this needs to be addressed. Justin has went from being hyper to being on high alert and questioning the gov. My suggestion would be to family members, watch your vet with PTSD. I know it is big news, but I wouldn't keep the news playing as it may trigger them... Shawn

A collection of words on a Facebook page, but not just any old page. It was the page I had built, the one that had grown from the seeds of my need to do something meaningful in response to the situation I'd endured for so long and continue to endure. As that post from May 2 hints at, I knew that this wouldn't be the end of our troubles with PTSD. There would still be so much more to come as we continue our fight with the VA to get Justin's disability claim pushed through and as we continue to keep working in our house to make our lives better. It was closure in a way, but not the ending Justin thought it would be at first.

When the events of September 11, 2001 happened, I didn't know how I would be affected. But as September 11, 2011 approaches, I find this deep sense of satisfaction in me because this time I know a big change is coming with the release of this book on that day, and I'm hopeful the change will be good. I feel like I am reclaiming that day by making something good happen in my life to make up for all the bad that came my way from the first September 11th. By writing out my story, I was able to sort through my thoughts and get a grip on what was happening in my home. And now by sharing that story with the world, I'm hoping that my book will help other spouses like me figure out what they can do to help their family heal from the invisible wounds of war.

In our case, it almost doesn't matter what Justin did, or who he became under the influence of PTSD. All that matters is that we are together now and fixing it. Justin still has his good days and bad days, but that makes the good days all that much better. We still attend counseling at the Vet Center and Justin still gets medication from the VA to help him live with PTSD.

Sometimes I remember how that therapist described Justin as a square peg in a round hole. I used to think that it was only Justin who had to change, but now I realize we both do. It's like trying to turn him into a triangle-shaped peg to match a triangle-shaped hole. He may not be the man I married anymore, but I am also not the woman he married.

I wish I could say everything is perfect now and that we have no problems at all. But at least being together is manageable and we have a sense of hope that things will continue to get better going into the future, especially as we are now fighting for more than just ourselves. We have all those other families out there to help.

PTSD does not define us. I am no longer a victim. I have become a survivor of a survivor.

In 2004, Justin received a copy of the following letter to give to potential employers as a reference to his work skills. The letter clearly delineates the events that led to Justin's PTSD. It is part of the evidence that was submitted to the VA to support his claim for disability. As of the publishing of this book, Justin still has not been declared disabled.

20 May, 2004

From: Security Officer, USS GEORGE WASHINGTON (CVN-73)
To: Whom It May Concern

Subj: LETTER OF REFERENCE CONCERNING JUSTIN A. GOURLEY

1. Dear Sir or Madam, I am writing this letter to you as a positive reference for MR Gourley's application to your organization. Mr. Gourley faithfully and excellently performed his duties as a Security Armorer and Response Team Leader, while assigned to the U.S. Navy's Aircraft Carrier USS GEORGE WASHINGTON. His outstanding performance includes performing maintenance on and having accountability for 350 Small Arms Weapons valued at $350,000 and over 10,000 rounds of ammunition. Mr. Gourley ensured that our ship was ready to react to all threats, while deployed to the Northern Arabian Gulf and during the High Threat transit through the Suez Canal. As the response Team Leader, Gourley trained his team professionally making certain that they completed each task without incident. His thorough supervision resulted in USS GEORGE WASHINGTON achieving a reputation as one of the best security commands in the Navy.
2. I highly recommend Mr. Gourley for employment into your organization. He is a young intelligent person, who is willing to learn and adapt to any situation. I regret his decision to separate from the military but respect his decision and wish him success in his employment and future. He is a definite great find as an employee.

Very sincerely,

[signature]
Keith A. Tukes
Security Officer
USS GEORGE WASHINGTON (CVN-73)

TIMELINE

Before 1988

January 1988: Shawn and Justin meet.

June 2000: Justin enlists in the Navy.

October 12, 2000: Attack on USS Cole.

2001

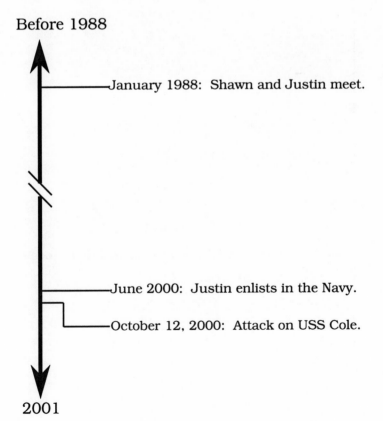

2000

September 11-15, 2001: Attacks on WTC and Pentagon, plane goes down in Pennsylvania. The USS Washington provides air defense for NYC. Justin moves from an Operations Specialist (RADAR) to Military Police.

December 2001: Shawn and Justin begin dating.

2002

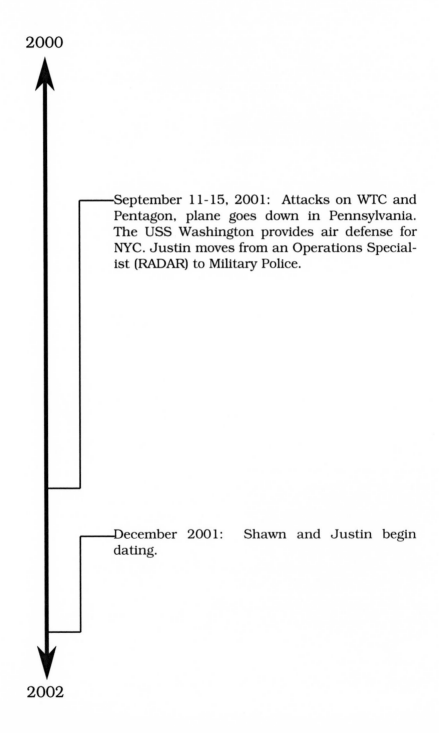

2001

June 2002: The USS Washington is deployed to the Mediterranean Sea and Arabian Gulf and participated in Operation Enduring Freedom.

October 2, 2002: 3 Doors Down performs on the USS Washington.

December 20, 2002: USS Washington returns to Norfolk, VA.

2003

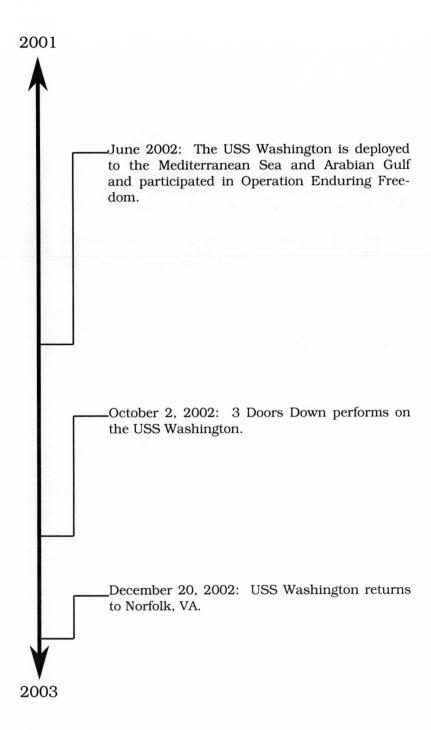

2002

January 24 - February 5, 2003: USS Washington runs carrier qualification in West Lant, Justin has to handle his first corpse on February 4.

February 14, 2003: Justin proposes to Shawn.

February, 2003: Shawn and Justin start marriage counseling at church.

February 25 - August 15, 2003: The USS Washington is docked for maintenance.

March, 2003: Justin undergoes anti-terrorism training.

March 28, 2003: Shawn and Justin elope.

June, 2003: Shawn and Justin buy a house in Evansville, IN.

September 11, 2003: Justin helps with the wounded in the aftermath of a mishap with an arrested landing on the USS Washington.

October, 2003: Shawn conceives Jesse.

November 21, 2003: Justin's shipmate was killed, and he had to handle the corpse.

2004

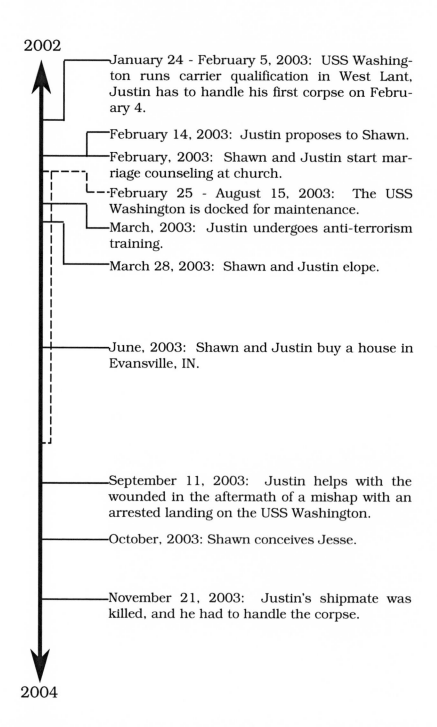

2003

January 20, 2004: The USS Washington is deployed to the Mediterranean Sea and Arabian Gulf to provide support for both Operation Enduring Freedom and Operation Iraqi Freedom.

March, 2004: Justin is on duty when the USS Washington is approached by an unidentified vessel while making a high-risk transit through the Suez Canal.

June, 2004: Justin returns home; his military service is complete.

July, 2004: Jesse is born. Justin begins to have nightmares.

August, 2004: Justin begins to exhibit road rage.

September, 2004: Justin begins working two jobs.

October, 2004: Justin's application to join the police force is rejected.

2005

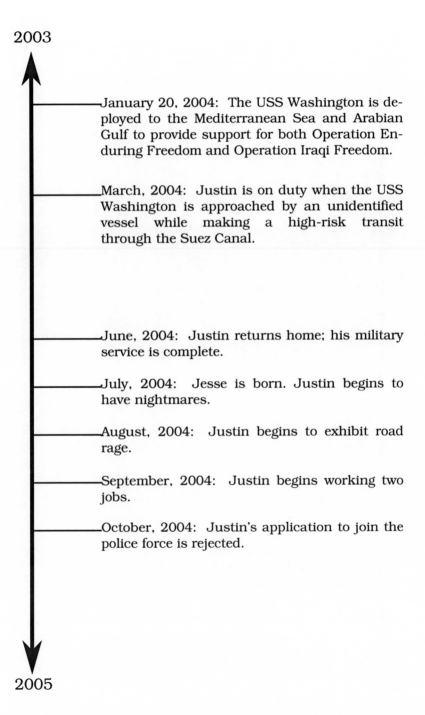

2004

May 2005: Justin begins work at Toyota.

June 2005: Justin pulls a gun on Shawn. The VA rejects Shawn's request for help.

August 2005: Shawn conceives Jaxson.

September 2005 - April 2006: Shawn begins to have trouble with kidney stones and has many visits to the hospital.

2006

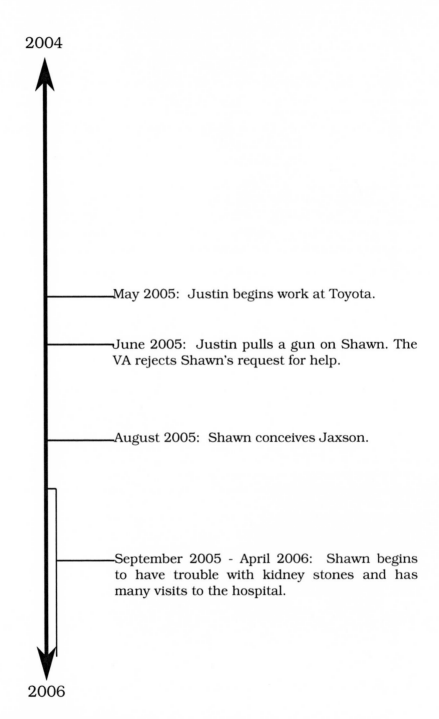

2005

April 2006: Jaxson is born.

May 2006: Jesse kicks a candle over and starts a house fire.

September 2006: Justin, Shawn, and the kids move back home.

October 2006: Justin launches Shawn across the kitchen during an argument. Shawn calls 911 but then tells the police everything is fine. Shawn calls the VA for help and is again rejected.

2007

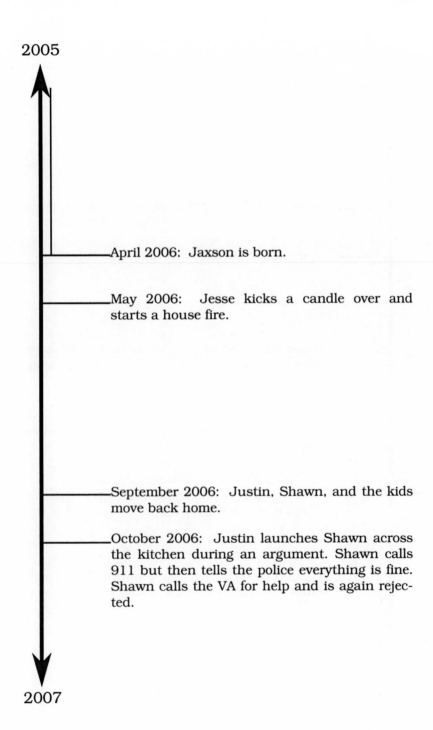

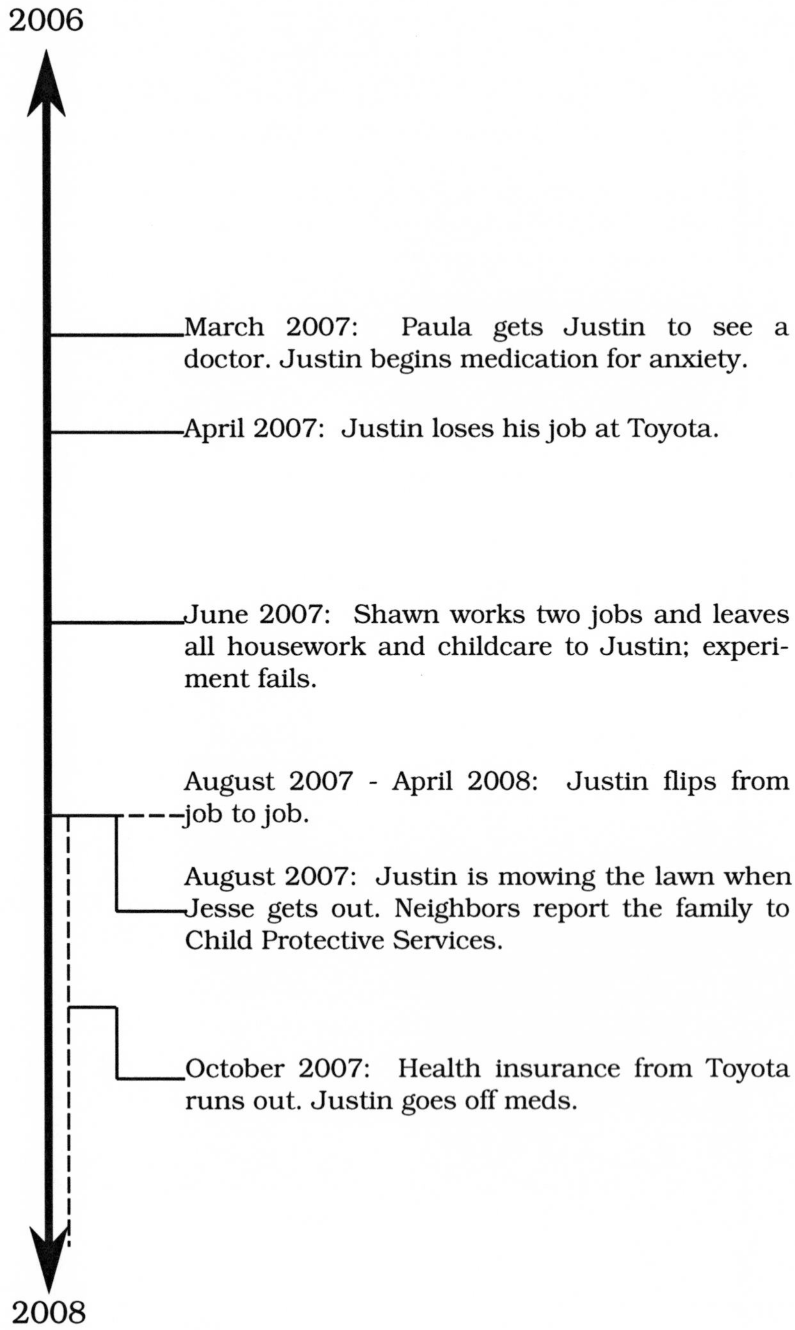
2006
March 2007: Paula gets Justin to see a doctor. Justin begins medication for anxiety.
April 2007: Justin loses his job at Toyota.
June 2007: Shawn works two jobs and leaves all housework and childcare to Justin; experiment fails.
August 2007 - April 2008: Justin flips from job to job.
August 2007: Justin is mowing the lawn when Jesse gets out. Neighbors report the family to Child Protective Services.
October 2007: Health insurance from Toyota runs out. Justin goes off meds.
2008

2007

January 2008: President Bush passes the National Defense Authorization Act of 2008 allowing for more help for OEF/OIF combat veterans.

April 2008: Justin gets a job as a machinist.

April 2008 - January 2009: Household is in constant turmoil.

2009

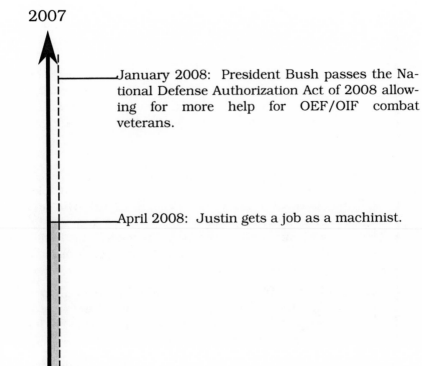

2008

January 2009: Shawn notices bruises on Jaxson. Justin flips out and slams a toy against the wall. Shawn calls one last time for help with the VA and this time gets assistance.

May 2009: Shawn speaks with her counselor about Secondary PTSD regarding her own and her daughter's behavior. Shawn and Justin start an Xbox 360 repair business from home. Jaxson's bruises turn out to be symptoms of a blood disorder.

June 2009: Shawn watches *Full Metal Jacket* and begins to understand what Justin went through in the Navy. Shawn and Justin file for Justin's disability. Justin gets laid off.

July 2009: Shawn has an emotional meltdown in a counseling session.

August 2009: The Vet Center counselor concludes her internship.

September 2009: Justin contracts the Superbug MRSA staph infection.

October 2009: Justin comes home and Shawn provides constant medical care. Shawn and Justin close the Xbox repair business. Shawn begins work on writing an Xbox DVD repair manual. The VA sends a letter requesting additional information for Justin's claims.

2010

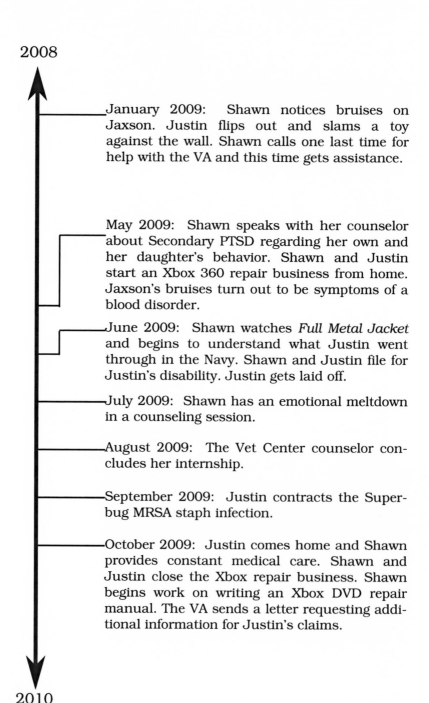

2009

January 2010: Shawn puts the Xbox repair manual up for sale. The VA sends a second request for info. The new Vet Center counselor arrives.

March 2010: Justin receives a denial letter for his VA disability claim. Justin stops going to counseling.

May 2010: Justin hits a pedestrian with his truck while driving around to blow off steam from an argument. Shawn moves herself and the kids into a camper; Justin follows.

June 2010: The police are called to check on Shawn and Justin's house for animal welfare. Justin gets a job and resumes seeing the Vet Center counselor.

July 2010: Shawn begins writing her mini-book on PTSD.

August 2010: Shawn launches the Military with PTSD™ Facebook Page. Justin gets fired.

September 2010: Justin gets a job and is fired again within a week. Shawn starts getting interview requests regarding her book on PTSD.

October 1, 2010: Shawn releases the free electronic mini-book of *The War at Home: One Family's Fight Against PTSD.*

November 2010: Shawn receives overwhelming positive response to her book from many directions. Shawn also has a TV interview and decides to put the book into print due to high demand.

December 2010: Justin tries to get involved with the Facebook page, but is not well received due to his portrayal in the mini-book.

2011

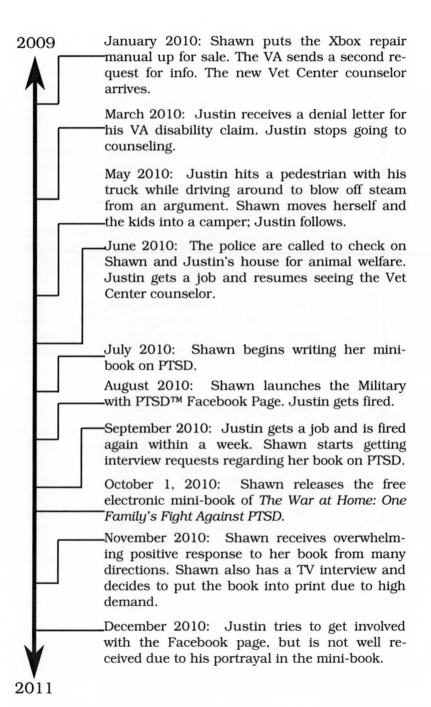

2010

January - March, 2011: Shawn is off the Facebook page for a couple months and Justin begins to field questions directly from the page members. At their request, he agrees to write a portion of the book from his point of view.

February - March, 2011: Shawn uses her time to work on the book and try to negotiate with publishers. Eventually, she decides to self-publish.

March 23, 2011: Shawn first speaks with Spring Lea Henry at The Grumpy Dragon. Within days, a contract is offered and they begin work on the full version of *The War at Home: One Family's Fight Against PTSD.*

April 30, 2011: Shawn is scheduled to speak at a benefit concert for incarcerated veterans. At the event, she meets other advocates for veterans and makes plans to collaborate with them in the future.

May 1, 2011: Osama bin Laden is shot to death in a Navy SEAL mission.

May 2, 2011: Shawn and the members of the Military with PTSD™ Facebook page have discussions about the realization that Bin Laden's death is not the end of the story for those with PTSD.

May 10, 2011: Shawn calls the VA's National Caregiver Support Line and fully accepts that her role in the future is to be an advocate for change on behalf of all military with PTSD and their spouses and families.

September 11, 2011: *The War at Home* is officially released.

Future

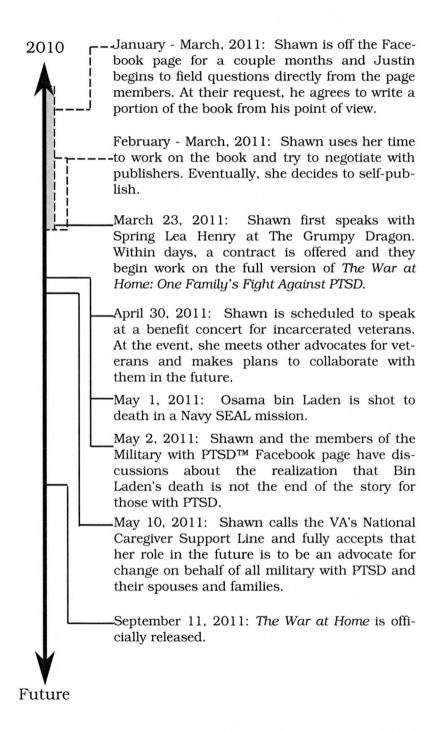

RESOURCES
(Annotated)

Books

England, Diane. *The Post-Traumatic Stress Disorder Relationship.* This book is an intensely clinical examination of the affects PTSD has on a relationship. It provides insight into the way PTSD affects attitudes and moods, including the dynamics of abuse. The text includes strategies for all aspects of a relationship, including that of parent and child.

Evans, Patricia:

Controlling People: How to Recognize, Understand, and Deal with People Who Try to Control You. Describes how trauma in a person's life can cause them to feel the need to control everything and everyone around them, which is a common symptom of PTSD. This book helps with recognizing that situation and how to cope with it.

The Verbally Abusive Relationship: How to Recognize It and How to Respond. This book helps victims of verbal abuse recognize the dynamics of dysfunction and talks abouts ways to respond to help break the cycle.

Grossman, Dave. *On Killing: The Psychological Cost of Learning to Kill in War and Society.* This is a very intimate look inside the mind of a soldier. The author explains how attitudes of hyper-protectiveness and violence are trained into becoming mindless habit rather than conscious thought. It's useful for spouses to understand what a vet might be thinking.

Lanham, Stephanie Laite. *Veterans and Families' Guide to Recovering from PTSD.* This book is routinely given to veterans and their spouses by therapists at Vet Centers to help them start to understand what is going on. It is a systematic break-down of the symptoms of PTSD in very plain language to make it easy for almost everyone to understand. The book also includes writings from veterans and families, resource for veterans, and a list of all the Vet Centers nationwide.

Orange, Cynthia. *Shock Waves.* This book is written in everyday language to help spouses understand how a veteran thinks. The author includes many anecdotes, including her own, as illustrations of her point-of-view. It's very useful in understanding the why of PTSD thinking.

Ruiz, Don Miguel. *The Four Agreements: A Practical Guide to Personal Freedom, A Toltec Wisdom Book.* This book teaches, among other good skills, the art of not taking things personally, which is very important to any relationship, but especially important when PTSD is altering behavior. It's short and written in plain English so that anyone can understand the powerful lessons it contains.

Seahorn, Anthony and Dr. Janet. *Tears of a Warrior.* This book details both sides of the PTSD story, giving the reader insight into the causes of the condition and ways to cope with someone who has it. Janet's advice is not clinical, despite her degree, but springs from the conditions in her own home. This is a very personal story as well as one that has helped thousands of families understand what is really going on inside the mind of veterans who suffer from PTSD.

Waddell, Marshēle Carter:

Hope for the Home Front: God's Timeless Encouragement for Today's Military Wife.

Hope for the Home Front: Winning the Emotional and Spiritual Battles of a Military Wife.

Hope for the Home Front Bible Study: Winning the Emotional and Spiritual Battles of a Military Wife.

When War Comes Home: Christ-centered Healing for Wives of Combat Veterans. (With Rev. Christopher B. Adsit.)

These books provide help for spouses of veterans with PTSD through the lens of Bible studies and a Christian perspective. There are guided exercises, recommended scripture, prayers, and suggestions for self-care while helping tending to the needs of a veteran with

PTSD. There is some very practical secular advice included as well. She covers the topic of abuse in depth, particularly the emotional abuse that is more subtle in a household where there is PTSD.

Websites and Phone Numbers

Citizens Soldiers, Inc.
http://www.citizenssoldiersinc.org/
This organization helps homeless veterans who have PTSD and help them get their lives back in order.

Family of a Vet
http://www.familyofavet.com/
This website is a clearing house of information to help veterans and their families deal with PTSD and TBI.

Give an Hour
http://www.giveanhour.org/
This organization helps US military personnel and their families who are dealing with issues pertaining to the conflicts in Iraq and Afghanistan.

Living with PTSD and TBI
http://www.armyreservistwife.blogspot
This blog is a breakdown of PTSD and TBI from the point of view of a spouse who is living through this situation. It is maintained regularly and gives a very honest depiction of the situation.

Military With PTSD™
http://militarywithptsd.com/
This is a page for veterans, spouses, family members, and friends to find help and resources for dealing with military personnel who have PTSD.

National Center for PTSD
http://www.ptsd.va.gov/
This website helps connect veterans with resources for dealing with PTSD.

National Domestic Violence Hotline:
1-800-799-7233
http://www.ndvh.org/

National Suicide Prevention Lifeline:
If you are in crisis, please call 911, go to your nearest Emergency Room, or call 1-800-273-TALK (1-800-273-8255) (Español 1-888-628-9454).
Veterans, press "1" after you call — or go to Veterans Suicide Prevention Hotline to chat live with a crisis counselor at any time of day or night.

Soldiers' Angels
http://www.soldiersangels.org/
This group helps organize volunteers to provide comfort and aid to soldiers, such as sending care packages and writing Christmas cards.

Talking with Heroes
http://www.talkingwith heroes.com
This website and radio show helps keep people up-to-date on what is happening in Iraq and Afghanistan as well as providing ongoing support to troops. Episodes of the show are also archived on YouTube.

LIST OF VETERANS' CENTERS

Please note that this list is subject to change as Vet Centers open, close, and relocate over time. When in doubt, please check the Department of Veterans Affairs website at www.va.gov.

Alabama

Birmingham Vet Center
1201 2nd Avenue South
Birmingham, AL 35233
Phone: 205-212-3122
Fax: 205-212-3123

Huntsville Vet Center
415 Church Street, Bldg H, Suite 101
Huntsville, AL 35801
Phone: 256-539-5775
Fax: 256-533-1973

Mobile Vet Center
2577 Government Blvd.
Mobile, AL 36606
Phone: 251-478-5906
Fax: 251-478-2237

Montgomery Vet Center
4405 Atlanta Highway
Montgomery, AL 36109
Phone: 334-273-7796
Fax: 334-277-8376
At the main number, choose extension 2263 or 4483

Alaska

Anchorage Vet Center
4201 Tudor Centre Drive, Suite 115
Anchorage, AK 99508
Phone: 907-563-6966
Fax: 907-561-7183

Fairbanks Vet Center
540 4th Ave., Suite 100
Fairbanks, AK 99701
Phone: 907-456-4238
Fax: 907-456-0475

Kenai Vet Center Satellite
Bldg. F, Suite 4 Red Diamond Ctr,
43335 Kalifornsky Beach Rd.
Soldotna, AK 99669
Phone: 907-260-7640
Fax: 907-260-7642

Wasilla Vet Center
851 E. West Point Drive Suite 111
Wasilla, AK 99654
Phone: 907-376-4318
Fax: 907-373-1883

Arizona

Chinle Mobile Vet Center
Navajo (Indn) Rt. 7
Chinle, AZ 86503
Phone: 928-674-3682
Fax: 928-674-5640

Chinle Vet Center Outstation
P.O. Box 1934
Chinle, AZ 86503
Phone: 928-674-3682
Fax: 928-674-5640

Hopi Vet Center Outstation 2
P.O. Box 929, 1 Main St.
Hotevilla, AZ 86030
Phone: 928-734-5166
Fax: 928-738-5531

Mesa Vet Center
1303 South Longmore, Suite 5
Mesa, AZ 85202
Phone: 480-610-6727
Fax: 480-464-3526

West Valley Vet Center
14050 N. 83rd Avenue Suite 170
Peoria, AZ 85381
Phone: 623-398-8854
Fax: 623-398-6478

Phoenix Vet Center
77 E. Weldon Suite 100
Phoenix, AZ 85012
Phone: 602-640-2981
Fax: 602-640-2967

Prescott Vet Center
3180 Stillwater Drive, Suite A
Prescott, AZ 86305
Phone: 928-778-3469
Fax: 928-776-6042

Tucson Vet Center
3055 N. First Avenue
Tucson, AZ 85719
Phone: 520-882-0333
Fax: 520-670-5862

Yuma Vet Center
3939 S. Ave SE suite 122
Yuma, AZ 85365
Phone: 928-271-8700
Fax: 928-304-7446

Arkansas

Fayetteville Vet Center
1416 N. College Ave.
Fayetteville, AR 72703
Phone: 479-582-7152
Fax: 479-251-1832

Little Rock Vet Center
201 W. Broadway St. Suite A
North Little Rock, AR 72114
Phone: 501-324-6395
Fax: 501-324-6928

California

Bakersfield Vet Center
2717 O Street
Bakersfield, CA 93301
Phone: 661-323-8387
Fax: 661-323-8387

Chula Vista Vet Center
180 Otay Lakes Road, Suite 108
Bonita, CA 91902-2439
Phone: 858-618-6534 Or 858-404-8380
Fax: 619-479-8539

Santa Cruz County Vet Center
1350 41st Ave Suite 102
Capitola, CA 95010
Phone: 831-464-4575
Fax: 831-464-6597

Chico Vet Center
280 Cohasset Road, Suite 100
Chico, CA 95928
Phone: 530-899-8549
Fax: 530-899-0581

Citrus Heights Vet Center
5650 Sunrise Blvd., Suite 150
Citrus Heights, CA 95610
Phone: 916-535-0420
Fax: 919-535-0419

San Bernardino Vet Center
1325 E. Cooley Drive, Suite 101
Colton, CA 92324
Phone: 909-801-5762
Fax: 909-801-5767

East Los Angeles Vet Center
5400 E. Olympic Blvd. #140
Commerce, CA 90022
Phone: 323-728-9966
Fax: 323-887-1082

Concord Vet Center
1899 Clayton Rd. Suite 140
Concord, CA 94520
Phone: 925-680-4526
Fax: 925-680-0410

Corona Vet Center
800 Magnolia Avenue Suite 110
Corona, CA 92879
Phone: 951-734-0525
Fax: 951-734-0063

West Los Angeles Vet Center
5730 Uplander Way Suite 100
Culver City, CA 90230
Phone: 310-641-0326
Fax: 310-641-2653

Redwoods Vet Center
2830 G Street, Suite A
Eureka, CA 95501
Phone: 707-444-8271
Fax: 707-444-8391

Fairfield: 4B Pacific Western Regional Office
420 Executive Court North Suite G
Fairfield, CA 94534
Phone: 707-646-2988
Fax: 707-646-2960

Fresno Vet Center
3636 North 1st St. Suite 112
Fresno, CA 93726
Phone: 559-487-5660
Fax: 559-487-5399

Orange County Vet Center
12453 Lewis St. Suite 101
Garden Grove, CA 92840
Phone: 714-776-0161
Fax: 714-748-4573

Los Angeles Veterans Resource Center
1045 W. Redondo Beach Blvd. Suite 150
Gardena, CA 90247
Phone: 310-767-1221
Fax: 310-767-1403

South Orange County Vet Center
26431 Crown Valley Parkway, Suite 100
Mission Viejo, CA 92691
Phone: 949-348-6700
Fax: 949-348-6719

Modesto Vet Center
1219 N. Carpenter Rd., Suite 12
Modesto, CA 95351
Phone: 209-569-0713
Fax: 209-569-0718

Oakland Vet Center
1504 Franklin St. Suite 200
Oakland, CA 94612
Phone: 510-763-3904
Fax: 510-763-5631

Antelope Valley Vet Center
38925 Trade Center Drive, Suite J
Palmdale, CA 93551
Phone: 661-267-1026
Fax: 661-267-2045

Peninsula Vet Center
2946 Broadway St.
Redwood City, CA 94062
Phone: 650-299-0672
Fax: 650-299-0677

Northbay Vet Center
6225 State Farm Drive Suite 101
Rohnert Park, CA 94928
Phone: 707-586-3295
Fax: 707-586-9055

Sacramento Vet Center
1111 Howe Avenue Suite #390
Sacramento, CA 95825
Phone: 916-566-7430
Fax: 916-566-7433

San Diego Vet Center
2790 Truxtun Road, Suite 130
San Diego, CA 92106
Phone: 858-642-1500
Fax: 619-294-2535

San Francisco Vet Center
505 Polk Street
San Francisco, CA 94102
Phone: 415-441-5051
Fax: 415-441-5092

San Jose Vet Center
278 North 2nd St.
San Jose, CA 95112
Phone: 408-993-0729
Fax: 408-993-0829

San Marcos Vet Center
One Civic Center Dr., Suite 140
San Marcos, CA 92069
Phone: 760-744-6914
Fax: 760-744-6919

Sepulveda Vet Center
9737 Haskell Ave.
Sepulveda, CA 91343
Phone: 818-892-9227
Fax: 818-892-0557

Temecula Vet Center
40935 County Center Drive, Suite A
Temecula, CA 92591
Phone: 951-302-4849
Fax: 951-296-0598

Ventura Vet Center
790 E. Santa Clara St. Suite 100
Ventura, CA 93001
Phone: 805-585-1860
Fax: 805-585-1864

High Desert Vet Center
15095 Amargosa Rd, Suite 107
Victorville, CA 92394
Phone: 760-261-5925
Fax: 760-241-7828

Colorado

Denver: 4A Western Mountain Regional Office
789 Sherman Street, Suite 570
Denver, CO 80203
Phone: 303-393-2897
Fax: 303-860-7614

Boulder Vet Center
2336 Canyon Blvd., Suite 103
Boulder, CO 80302
Phone: 303-440-7306
Fax: 303-449-3907

Colorado Springs Vet Center
602 South Nevada Avenue
Colorado Springs, CO 80903
Phone: 719-471-9992
Fax: 719-632-7571

Denver Vet Center
7465 East First Avenue Suite B
Denver, CO 80230
Phone: 303-326-0645
Fax: 303-326-0715

Ft. Collins Vet Center Outstation
2509 Research Blvd
Ft. Collins, CO 80526
Phone: 970-221-5176
Fax: 970-482-9428

Grand Junction Vet Center
2472 F. Road Unit 16
Grand Junction, CO 81505
Phone: 970-245-4156
Fax: 970-245-7623

Pueblo (Colorado Springs Vet Center)
509 E. 13th St., Rm 18
Pueblo, CO 81001
Phone: 719-546-6666 X 133

Connecticut

Danbury Vet Center
457 North Main St.
Danbury, CT 06811
Phone: 203-790-4000 Or 203-790-4020

Norwich Vet Center
2 Cliff St.
Norwich, CT 06360
Phone: 860-887-1755
Fax: 860-887-2444

Hartford Vet Center
25 Elm Street, Suite A
Rocky Hill, CT 06067
Phone: 860-563-8800
Fax: 860-563-8805

New Haven Vet Center
141 Captain Thomas Blvd.
West Haven, CT 06516
Phone: 203-932-9899
Fax: 203-937-9419

Delaware

Wilmington Vet Center
VAMC, Bldg 3 1601 Kirkwood Highway
Wilmington, DE 19805
Phone: 302-994-1660
Fax: 302-633-5250

District of Columbia

Washington DC Vet Center
1250 Taylor St, NW
Washington, DC 20011
Phone: 202-726-5212
Fax: 202-726-8968

Florida

Bay Pines: 3A Southeast Regional Office
RCS, 10B/RC3A VA Medical Center, Bldg. T203
Bay Pines, FL 33744
Phone: 727-398-9343
Fax: 727-398-9444

Clearwater Vet Center
29259 US Hwy 19 North
Clearwater, FL 33761
Phone: 727-549-3600
Fax: 727-299-6701

Pompano Beach Vet Center
2300 W Sample Rd.
Coral Springs, FL 33073
Phone: 954-357-5555
Fax: 954-357-5710

Daytona Beach Vet Center
1620 Mason Ave., Suite C
Daytona Beach, FL 32117
Phone: 321-366-6600
Fax: 386-274-5700

Fort Lauderdale Vet Center
713 NE 3rd Ave.
Ft. Lauderdale, FL 33304
Phone: 954-356-7926 Fax: 954-356-7609

Ft. Myers Vet Center
4110 Center Pointe Drive, Unit 204
Ft. Myers, FL 33916
Phone: 239-479-4401
Fax: 239-277-5817

Gainesville Vet Center
105 NW 75th Street, Suite #2
Gainesville, FL 32607
Phone: 352-331-1408
Fax: 352-331-1962

Palm Beach Vet Center
4996 10th Ave North Suite 6
Greenacres, FL 33463
Phone: 561-422-1201
Fax: 561-439-5877

Jacksonville Vet Center
300 East State St., Suite J
Jacksonville, FL 32202
Phone: 904-232-3621
Fax: 904-232-3167

Jupiter Vet Center
6650 W. Indiantown Rd., Suite 120
Jupiter, FL 33458
Phone: 561-422-1220
Fax: 561-746-1458

Key Largo Vet Center Outstation
105662 Overseas Hwy.
Key Largo, FL 33037
Phone: 305-451-0164
Fax: 305-451-4864

Melbourne Vet Center
2098 Sarno Road
Melbourne, FL 32935
Phone: 321-254-3410
Fax: 321-254-9138

Miami Vet Center
8280 NW 27th St Suite 511
Miami, FL 33122
Phone: 305-718-3712
Fax: 305-718-8712

Orlando Vet Center
5575 S. Semoran Blvd. #36
Orlando, FL 32822
Phone: 407-857-2800
Fax: 407-857-5005

Pensacola Vet Center
4501 Twin Oaks Drive, Suite 104
Pensacola, FL 32506
Phone: 850-456-5886
Fax: 850-456-9403

Sarasota Vet Center
4801 Swift Rd. Suite A
Sarasota, FL 34231
Phone: 941-927-8285
Fax: 941-927-8307

St. Petersburg Vet Center
2880 1st Ave. North
St. Petersburg, FL 33713
Phone: 727-893-3791
Fax: 727-893-3210

Tallahassee Vet Center
548 Bradford Road
Tallahassee, FL 32303
Phone: 850-942-8810
Fax: 850-942-8814

Tampa Vet Center
8900 N Armenia Ave. #312
Tampa, FL 33604
Phone: 813-228-2621
Fax: 813-228-2868

Georgia

Atlanta Vet Center
1440 Dutch Valley Place, Suite 1100 Box 55
Atlanta, GA 30324
Phone: 404-347-7264
Fax: 404-347-7274

Lawrenceville Vet Center
930 River Centre Place
Lawrenceville, GA 30043
Phone: 770-963-1809
Fax: 770-963-6393

Macon Vet Center
750 Riverside Drive
Macon, GA 31201
Phone: 478-477-3813
Fax: 478-746-702

Marietta Vet Center
40 Dodd St., Suite 700
Marietta, GA 30060
Phone: 404-327-4954
Fax: 770-419-1314

Savannah Vet Center
308 A Commercial Dr
Savannah, GA 31406
Phone: 912-652-4097
Fax: 912-692-0250

Hawaii

Hilo Vet Center
126 Pu'uhonu Way Suite 2
Hilo, HI 96720
Phone: 808-969-3833
Fax: 808-969-2025

Honolulu Vet Center
1680 Kapiolani Blvd. Suite F-3
Honolulu, HI 96814
Phone: 808-973-8387
Fax: 808-973-5295

Kailua-Kona Vet Center
73-4976 Kamanu St., Suite 207
Kailua-Kona, HI 96740
Phone: 808-329-0574
Fax: 808-329-2799

Kauai Vet Center
3-3367 Kuhio Hwy. Ste #101
Lihue, HI 96766
Phone: 808-246-1163
Fax: 808-246-4625

Maui Vet Center
35 Lunalilo Street, Suite #101
Wailuku, HI 96793
Phone: 808-242-8557
Fax: 808-242-8559

Idaho

Boise Vet Center
5440 Franklin Road Suite 100
Boise, ID 83705
Phone: 208-342-3612
Fax: 208-342-0327

Pocatello Vet Center
1800 Garrett Way
Pocatello, ID 83201
Phone: 208-232-0316
Fax: 208-232-6258

Illinois

DuPage County Vet Center
750 Shoreline Drive, Suite 150
Aurora, IL 60504
Phone: 630-585-1853
Fax: 630-585-1956

Chicago Veterans Resource Center
7731 S. Halsted Street
Chicago, IL 60620-2412
Phone: 773-962-3740
Fax: 773-962-3750

Chicago Heights Vet Center
1600 Halsted Street
Chicago Heights, IL 60411
Phone: 708-754-0340
Fax: 708-754-9882

East St. Louis Vet Center
1265 N. 89th Street Suite 5
East St. Louis, IL 62203
Phone: 618-397-6602
Fax: 618-397-6541

Evanston Vet Center
565 Howard St.
Evanston, IL 60202
Phone: 847-332-1019
Fax: 847-332-1024

Quad Cities Vet Center
1529 46th Avenue #6
Moline, IL 61265
Phone: 309-762-6954
Fax: 309-762-8298

Oak Park Vet Center
155 S. Oak Park Avenue
Oak Park, IL 60302
Phone: 708-383-3225
Fax: 708-383-3247

Peoria Vet Center
3310 N. Prospect Road
Peoria, IL 61603
Phone: 309-688-2170
Fax: 309-688-2811

Rockford Vet Center Outstation
4960 E. State St. #3
Rockford, IL 61108
Phone: 815-395-1276
Fax: 815-395-1280

Springfield Vet Center
1227 S. Ninth Street
Springfield, IL 62703
Phone: 217-492-4955
Fax: 217-492-4963

Indiana

Evansville Vet Center
311 N. Weinbach Avenue
Evansville, IN 47711
Phone: 812-473-5993
Fax: 812-473-4028

Fort Wayne Vet Center
528 W. Berry Street
Fort Wayne, IN 46802
Phone: 260-460-1456
Fax: 206-460-1390

Indianapolis Vet Center
3833 N. Meridian Street, Suite 120
Indianapolis, IN 46208
Phone: 317-988-1600
Fax: 317-988-1617

Gary Area Vet Center
6505 Broadway Ave.
Merrillville, IN 46410
Phone: 219-736-5633
Fax: 219-736-5937

Iowa

Cedar Rapids Vet Center Satellite
1642 42nd Street NE
Cedar Rapids, IA 52402
Phone: 319-378-0016
Fax: 319-378-8145

Des Moines Vet Center
2600 Martin Luther King Pkwy
Des Moines, IA 50310
Phone: 515-284-4929
Fax: 515-277-4949

Sioux City Vet Center
1551 Indian Hills Drive Suite 214
Sioux City, IA 51104
Phone: 712-255-3808
Fax: 712-255-3725

Kansas

Manhattan Vet Center
205 South 4th Street, Suite B
Manhattan, KS 66502
Phone: 785-587-8257
Fax: 785-539-4982

Wichita Vet Center
251 N. Water St.
Wichita, KS 67202
Phone: 316-685-2221
Fax: 316-265-0910

Kentucky

Lexington Vet Center
301 E. Vine Street Suite C
Lexington, KY 40507
Phone: 859-253-0717
Fax: 859-281-4801

Louisville Vet Center
1347 S. Third Street
Louisville, KY 40208
Phone: 502-634-1916
Fax: 502-625-7082

Louisiana

Rapides Parish Vet Center
5803 Coliseum Blvd., Sute D
Alexandria, LA 70303
Phone: 318-466-4327
Fax: 318-427-8044

Baton Rouge Vet Center
5207 Essen Lane, Suite 2
Baton Rouge, LA 70809
Phone: 225-757-0042
Fax: 225-757-0054

New Orleans Veterans Resource Center
2200 Veterans Blvd. Suite 114
Kenner, LA 70062
Phone: 504-464-4743
Fax: 504-464-6710

Shreveport Vet Center
2800 Youree Dr. Bldg. 1, Suite 105
Shreveport, LA 71104
Phone: 318-861-1776
Fax: 318-868-1788

Maine

Bangor Vet Center
368 Harlow St. In-Town Plaza
Bangor, ME 04401
Phone: 207-947-3391
Fax: 207-941-8195

Caribou Vet Center
456 York Street York Street Complex
Caribou, ME 04736
Phone: 207-496-3900
Fax: 207-493-6773

Lewiston Vet Center
Parkway Complex 29 Westminster St.
Lewiston, ME 04240
Phone: 207-783-0068
Fax: 207-783-3505

Portland Vet Center
475 Stevens Ave.
Portland, ME 04103
Phone: 207-780-3584
Fax: 207-780-3545

Sanford Vet Center
628 Main Street
Springvale, ME 04083
Phone: 207-490-1513
Fax: 207-490-1609

Maryland

Readjustment Counseling Service, Mid-Atlantic Region
305 W. Chesapeake Ave., Suite 300
Towson, MD 21204
Phone: 410-828-6619
Fax: 410-962-5151

Aberdeen Vet Center Outstation 2
223 W. Bel Air Avenue
Aberdeen, MD 21001
Phone: 410-272-6771
Fax: 410-297-9041

Annapolis Vet Center
100 Annapolis Street, Suite 102
Annapolis, MD 21401
Phone: 410-605-7826
Fax: 410-267-0129

Baltimore Vet Center
1777 Reisterstown Road Suite 199
Baltimore, MD 21208
Phone: 410-764-9400
Fax: 410-764-7780

Silver Spring Vet Center
10411 Motor City Drive, 5th Floor
Bethesda, MD 20817
Phone: 240-395-1425
Fax: 240-395-1424

Cambridge Vet Center Outstation 1
830 Chesapeake Drive
Cambridge, MD 21613
Phone: 410-228-6305
Fax: 410-901-4011

Elkton Vet Center
103 Chesapeake Blvd. Suite A
Elkton, MD 21921
Phone: 410-392-4485
Fax: 410-392-6381

Massachusetts

Boston Vet Center
665 Beacon St. Suite 100
Boston, MA 02215
Phone: 617-424-0665
Fax: 617-424-0254

Brockton Vet Center
1041L Pearl St.
Brockton, MA 02301
Phone: 508-580-2730
Fax: 508-586-8414

Hyannis Vet Center
474 West Main Street
Hyannis, MA 02601
Phone: 508-778-0124
Fax: 508-775-3014

Lowell Vet Center
10 George Street, Gateway Center
Lowell, MA 01852
Phone: 978-453-1151
Fax: 978-441-1271

New Bedford Vet Center
468 North St.
New Bedford, MA 02740
Phone: 508-999-6920
Fax: 508-997-3348

Springfield Vet Center
1985 Main St. Northgate Plaza
Springfield, MA 01103
Phone: 413-737-5167
Fax: 413-733-0537

Worcester Vet Center
691 Grafton Street
Worcester, MA 01604
Phone: 508-753-7902
Fax: 508-753-4296

Michigan

Macomb County Vet Center
42621 Garfield Rd. Suite 105
Clinton Township, MI 48038-5031
Phone: 586-412-0107
Fax: 586-412-0196

Dearborn Vet Center
2881 Monroe Street Suite 100
Dearborn, MI 48124
Phone: 313-277-1428
Fax: 313-277-5471

Detroit Vet Center
4161 Cass Avenue
Detroit, MI 48201
Phone: 313-831-6509
Fax: 313-831-6919

Escanaba Vet Center
3500 Ludington Street, Suite # 110
Escanaba , MI 49829
Phone: 906-233-0244
Fax: 906-233-0217

Grand Rapids Vet Center
2050 Breton Rd SE
Grand Rapids, MI 49546
Phone: 616-285-5795
Fax: 616-285-5898

Pontiac Vet Center
44200 Woodward Avenue, Suite 108
Pontiac, MI 48341
Phone: 248-874-1015
Fax: 248-874-0813

Saginaw Vet Center
4048 Bay Road
Saginaw, MI 48603
Phone: 989-321-4650
Fax: 989-791-7507

Traverse City Vet Center
3766 N US 31 South
Traverse, MI 49684
Phone: 231-935-0051
Fax: 231-935-0071

Minnesota

Brooklyn Park Vet Center
7001 78th Avenue North, Suite 300
Brooklyn Park, MN 55445
Phone: 763-503-2220
Fax: 763-503-6179

Duluth Vet Center
405 E. Superior Street
Duluth, MN 55802
Phone: 218-722-8654
Fax: 218-723-8212

St. Paul Veterans Resource Center
550 County Road D, Suite 10
New Brighton, MN 55112
Phone: 651-644-4022
Fax: 651-917-2555

Mississippi

Biloxi Vet Center
288 Veterans Ave
Biloxi, MS 39531
Phone: 228-388-9938
Fax: 228-388-9253

Jackson Vet Center
1755 Lelia Dr. Suite 104
Jackson, MS 39216
Phone: 601-965-5727
Fax: 601-965-4023

Missouri

Columbia Vet Center
4040 Rangeline Road, Suite 105
Columbia, MO 65202
Phone: 573-814-6206
Fax: 573-814-2608

Kansas City Vet Center
301 East Armour Blvd Suite 305
Kansas City, MO 64111
Phone: 816-753-1866
Fax: 816-753-2328

Springfield, MO Vet Center
3616 S. Campbell
Springfield, MO 65807
Phone: 417-881-4197
Fax: 417-881-4932

2 Central Regional Office
2122 Kratky Rd.
St. Louis, MO 63114
Phone: 314-426-5864
Fax: 314-426-4725

St. Louis Vet Center
2901 Olive
St. Louis, MO 63103
Phone: 314-531-5355
Fax: 314-533-2796

Montana

Billings Vet Center
1234 Ave. C
Billings, MT 59102
Phone: 406-657-6071
Fax: 406-657-6603

Great Falls Vet Center
615 2nd Avenue North
Great Falls, MT 59401
Phone: 406-452-9048
Fax: 406-452-9053

Kalispell Vet Center
690 North Meridian Road, Suite 101
Kalispell, MT 59901
Phone: 406-257-7308
Fax: 406-257-7312

Missoula Vet Center
500 N. Higgins Avenue, Suite 202
Missoula, MT 59802
Phone: 406-721-4918
Fax: 406-329-3006

Nebraska

Lincoln Vet Center
3119 O Street, Suite A
Lincoln, NE 68510
Phone: 402-476-9736
Fax: 402-476-2431

Omaha Vet Center
2428 Cuming Street
Omaha, NE 68131-1600
Phone: 402-346-6735
Fax: 402-346-6020

Nevada

Henderson Vet Center
400 North Stephanie, Suite 180
Henderson, NV 89014
Phone: 702-791-9100
Fax: 702-433-5713

Las Vegas Vet Center
1919 S. Jones Blvd., Suite A
Las Vegas, NV 89146
Phone: 702-251-7873
Fax: 702-251-7812

Reno Vet Center
1155 W. 4th Street Suite 101
Reno, NV 89503
Phone: 775-323-1294
Fax: 775-322-8123

New Hampshire

1A Northeast Regional Office
15 Dartmouth Drive, Suite 204
Auburn, NH 03032
Phone: 603-623-4204
Fax: 603-623-5541

Berlin Vet Center
515 Main Street
Gorham, NH 03581
Phone: 603-752-2571
Fax: 603-752-3618

Manchester Vet Center
103 Liberty St.
Manchester, NH 03104
Phone: 603-668-7060
Fax: 603-666-7404

New Jersey

Bloomfield: Newark Vet Center
2 Broad St. Suite 703
Bloomfield, NJ 07003
Phone: 973-748-0980
Fax: 973-743-0380

Trenton Vet Center
934 Parkway Ave. Suite 201
Ewing, NJ 08618
Phone: 609-882-5744
Fax: 609-882-5743

Lakewood Vet Center
1255 Route 70; Unit 32N, Parkway Seventy Plaza
Lakewood, NJ 08701
Phone: 732-905-0327 Or 732-905-0327
Fax: 732-905-0329

Secaucus Vet Center
110A Meadowlands Parkway, Suite 102
Secaucus, NJ 07094
Phone: 201-223-7787
Fax: 201-223-7708

Ventnor Vet Center
6601 Ventnor Ave. Suite 105, Ventnor Bldg.
Ventnor, NJ 08406
Phone: 609-487-8387
Fax: 609-487-8910

New Mexico

Albuquerque Vet Center
1600 Mountain Road NW
Albuquerque, NM 87104
Phone: 505-346-6562
Fax: 505-346-6572

Farmington Vet Center Satellite
4251 E. Main Suite B
Farmington, NM 87402
Phone: 505-327-9684
Fax: 505-327-9519

Las Cruces Vet Center
230 S. Water Street
Las Cruces, NM 88001
Phone: 575-523-9826
Fax: 575-523-9827

Sante Fe Vet Center
2209 Brothers Road Suite 110
Santa Fe, NM 87505
Phone: 505-988-6562
Fax: 505-988-6564

New York

Albany Vet Center
17 Computer Drive West
Albany, NY 12205
Phone: 518-626-5130
Fax: 518-458-8613

Babylon Vet Center
116 West Main St.
Babylon, NY 11702
Phone: 631-661-3930
Fax: 631-422-5677

Binghamton Vet Center
53 Chenango Street
Binghamtom, NY 13901
Phone: 866-716-8213
Fax: 607-722-0143

Bronx Vet Center
2471 Morris Ave., Suite 1A
Bronx, NY 10468
Phone: 718-367-3500
Fax: 718-364-6867

Brooklyn Veterans Resource Center
25 Chapel St. Suite 604
Brooklyn, NY 11201
Phone: 718-624-2765
Fax: 718-624-3323

Buffalo Vet Center
564 Franklin Street 2nd Floor
Buffalo, NY 14202
Phone: 716-882-0505
Fax: 716-882-0525

Nassau Vet Center
970 South Broadway
Hicksville, NY 11801
Phone: 516-348-0088 Or 516-348-0088
Fax: 516-572-8580

Middletown Vet Center
726 East Main Street, Suite 203
Middletown, NY 10940
Phone: 845-342-9917
Fax: 845-343-8655

Harlem Vet Center
2279 - 3rd Avenue, 2nd Floor
New York, NY 10035
Phone: 212-426-2200
Fax: 212-426-8273

Manhattan Vet Center
32 Broadway 2nd Floor - Suite 200
New York, NY 10004
Phone: 212-742-9591
Fax: 212-742-9593

Rochester Vet Center
1867 Mount Hope Ave.
Rochester, NY 14620
Phone: 585-232-5040
Fax: 585-232-5072

Staten Island Vet Center
150 Richmond Terrace
Staten Island, NY 10301
Phone: 718-816-4499
Fax: 718-816-6899

Syracuse Vet Center
716 East Washington St. Suite 101
Syracuse, NY 13210
Phone: 315-478-7127
Fax: 315-478-7209

Watertown Vet Center
210 Court Street
Watertown, NY 13601
Phone: 866-610-0358
Fax: 315-782-0491

White Plains Vet Center
300 Hamilton Ave. 1st floor
White Plains, NY 10601
Phone: 914-682-6250
Fax: 914-682-6263

Queens Vet Center
75-10B 91 Ave.
Woodhaven, NY 11421
Phone: 718-296-2871
Fax: 718-296-4660

North Carolina

Charlotte Vet Center
2114 Ben Craig Dr., Suite 300
Charlotte, NC 28262
Phone: 704-549-8025
Fax: 704-549-8261

Fayetteville Vet Center
4140 Ramsey St. Suite 110
Fayetteville, NC 28311
Phone: 910-488-6252
Fax: 910-488-5589

Greensboro Vet Center
2009 S. Elm-Eugene St.
Greensboro, NC 27406
Phone: 336-333-5366
Fax: 336-333-5046

Greenville, NC Vet Center
1021 W.H. Smith Blvd., Suite A 100
Greenville, NC 27834
Phone: 252-355-7920
Fax: 252-756-7045

Raleigh Vet Center
1649 Old Louisburg Rd.
Raleigh, NC 27604
Phone: 919-856-4616
Fax: 919-856-4617

North Dakota

Bismarck Vet Center Outstation
1684 Capital Way
Bismarck, ND 58501
Phone: 701-224-9751
Fax: 701-223-5150

Fargo Vet Center
3310 Fiechtner Drive. Suite 100
Fargo, ND 58103-8730
Phone: 701-237-0942
Fax: 701-237-5734

Minot Vet Center
1400 20th Avenue SW
Minot, ND 58701
Phone: 701-852-0177
Fax: 701-852-5225

Ohio

Cincinnati Vet Center
801B W. 8th St. Suite 126
Cincinnati, OH 45203
Phone: 513-763-3500
Fax: 513-763-3505

Cleveland Heights Vet Center
2022 Lee Road
Cleveland, OH 44118
Phone: 216-932-8471
Fax: 216-932-1781

McCafferty Vet Center Outstation
4242 Lorain Avenue Suite 201
Cleveland, OH 44113
Phone: 216-939-0784
Fax: 216-939-0276

Columbus Vet Center
30 Spruce Street
Columbus, OH 43215
Phone: 614-257-5550
Fax: 614-257-5551

Dayton Vet Center
6th Floor, East Medical Plaza
627 Edwin C. Moses Blvd.
Dayton, OH 45408
Phone: 937-461-9150
Fax: 937-461-4574

Parma Vet Center
5700 Pearl Road Suite 102
Parma, OH 44129
Phone: 440-845-5023
Fax: 440-845-5024

Toledo Vet Center
1565 S. Byrne Road, Suite 104
Toledo, OH 43614
Phone: 419-213-7533
Fax: 419-380-9583
Toll Free 1-888-988-4883

Oklahoma

Lawton Vet Center
1016 SW C Avenue, Suite B
Lawton, OK 73501
Phone: 580-585-5880
Fax: 580-585-5890

Oklahoma City Vet Center
1024 NW 47th St. Suite B
Oklahoma City, OK 73118
Phone: 405-456-5184
Fax: 405-521-1794

Tulsa Vet Center
1408 S. Harvard Ave.
Tulsa, OK 74112
Phone: 918-748-5105
Fax: 918-748-5107

Oregon

Central Oregon Vet Center
1645 Forbes Rd. Suite 105
Bend, OR 97701
Phone: 541-749-2112
Fax: 541-647-5282

Eugene Vet Center
1255 Pearl Street Suite 200
Eugene, OR 97402
Phone: 541-465-6918
Fax: 541-465-6656

Grants Pass Vet Center
211 S.E. 10th St.
Grants Pass, OR 97526
Phone: 541-479-6912
Fax: 541-474-4589

Portland Vet Center
8383 N.E. Sandy Blvd. Suite #110
Portland, OR 97220
Phone: 503-273-5370
Fax: 503-273-5377

Salem Vet Center
617 Chemeketa St., NE Suite 100
Salem, OR 97301
Phone: 503-362-9911
Fax: 503-364-2534

Pennsylvania

Bucks County Vet Center
2 Canal's End Plaza, Suite 201B
Bristol, PA 19007
Phone: 215-823-4590

DuBois Vet Center
100 Meadow Lane, Suite 8
DuBois, PA 15801
Phone: 814-372-2095
Fax: 814-940-6511

Erie Vet Center
Renaissance Centre 1001 State St., Suite 102
Erie, PA 16501
Phone: 814-453-7955
Fax: 814-456-5464

Harrisburg Vet Center
1500 N. Second Street Suite 2
Harrisburg, PA 17102
Phone: 717-782-3954
Fax: 717-782-3791

Lancaster Vet Center
1817 Olde Homestead Lane
Lancaster, PA 17601
Phone: 717-283-0735

McKeesport Veterans Resource Center
2001 Lincoln Way
McKeesport, PA 15131
Phone: 412-678-7704
Fax: 412-678-7780

Montgomery County Vet Center
320 E. Johnson Hwy, Suite 201
Norristown, PA 19401
Phone: 215-823-5245
Fax: 610-272-2198

Philadelphia Vet Center
801 Arch Street Suite 102
Philadelphia, PA 19107
Phone: 215-627-0238
Fax: 215-597-6362

Philadelphia Vet Center NE
101 E. Olney Avenue
Philadelphia, PA 19120
Phone: 215-924-4670
Fax: 215-224-3252

Pittsburgh Vet Center
2500 Baldwick Rd
Pittsburgh, PA 15205
Phone: 412-920-1765
Fax: 412-920-1769

Scranton Vet Center
1002 Pittston Ave.
Scranton, PA 18505
Phone: 570-344-2676
Fax: 570-344-6794

Williamsport Vet Center
49 E. Fourth Street Suite 104
Williamsport, PA 17701
Phone: 570-327-5281
Fax: 570-322-4542

Rhode Island

Providence Vet Center
2038 Warwick Ave
Warwick, RI 02889
Phone: 401-739-0167
Fax: 401-739-7705

South Carolina

Columbia Vet Center
1513 Pickens St.
Columbia, SC 29201
Phone: 803-765-9944
Fax: 803-799-6267

Greenville, SC Vet Center
14 Lavinia Ave.
Greenville, SC 29601
Phone: 864-271-2711
Fax: 864-370-3655

Charleston Vet Center
5603-A Rivers Ave.
N. Charleston, SC 29406
Phone: 843-789-7000
Fax: 843-566-0232

South Dakota

Pine Ridge Vet Center Outstation
P.O. Box 910 105 E. Hwy 18
Martin, SD 57747
Phone: 605-685-1300
Fax: 605-685-1406

Rapid City Vet Center
621 6th St, Suite 101
Rapid City, SD 57701
Phone: 605-348-0077
Fax: 605-348-0878

Sioux Falls Vet Center
601 S. Cliff Ave. Suite C
Sioux Falls, SD 57104
Phone: 605-330-4552
Fax: 605-330-4554

Tennessee

Chattanooga Vet Center
951 Eastgate Loop Road Bldg. 5700 - Suite 300
Chattanooga, TN 37411
Phone: 423-855-6570
Fax: 423-855-6575

Johnson City Vet Center
1615A Market St.
Johnson City, TN 37604
Phone: 423-928-8387
Fax: 423-928-6320

Knoxville Vet Center
2817 E. Magnolia Ave.
Knoxville, TN 37914
Phone: 865-545-4680
Fax: 865-545-4198

Memphis Vet Center
1407 Union Ave., Suite 410
Memphis, TN 38104
Phone: 901-544-0173
Fax: 901-544-0179

Nashville Vet Center
1420 Donelson Pike Suite A-5
Nashville, TN 37217
Phone: 615-366-1220
Fax: 615-366-1351

Texas

Dallas: 3B South Central Regional Office
4500 S. Lancaster Rd. Building 69
Dallas, TX 75216
Phone: 214-857-1254
Fax: 214-462-4944

Taylor County Vet Center
400 Oak St.
Abilene, TX 79602
Phone: 325-674-1328

Amarillo Vet Center
3414 Olsen Blvd. Suite E
Amarillo, TX 79109
Phone: 806-354-9779
Fax: 806-351-1104

Austin Vet Center
1110 West William Cannon Dr. Suite 301
Austin, TX 78745
Phone: 512-416-1314
Fax: 512-416-7019

Corpus Christi Vet Center
4646 Corona Suite 250
Corpus Christi, TX 78411
Phone: 361-854-9961
Fax: 361-854-4730

Dallas Vet Center
10501 N. Central Suite 213
Dallas, TX 75231
Phone: 214-361-5896
Fax: 214-655-2249

El Paso Vet Center
1155 Westmoreland Suite 121
El Paso, TX 79925
Phone: 915-772-0013
Fax: 915-772-3983

Ft. Worth Vet Center
1305 W. Magnolia St. Suite B
Ft. Worth, TX 76104
Phone: 817-921-9095
Fax: 817-921-9438

Killeen Heights Vet Center
302 Millers Crossing, Suite #4
Harker Heights, TX 76548
Phone: 254-953-7100
Fax: 254-953-7120

Harris County Vet Center
14300 Cornerstone Village Dr., Suite 110
Houston, TX 77014
Phone: 713-578-4002
Fax: 281-583-8800

Houston Vet Center
2990 Richmond Suite 325
Houston, TX 77098
Phone: 713-523-0884
Fax: 713-523-4513

Houston Vet Center (Veterans Resource Center)
701 N. Post Oak Road Suite 102
Houston, TX 77024
Phone: 713-682-2288
Fax: 713-682-7818

Laredo Vet Center
6020 McPherson Road Suite 1A
Laredo, TX 78041
Phone: 956-723-4680
Fax: 956-723-9144

Lubbock Vet Center
3208 34th St.
Lubbock, TX 79410
Phone: 806-792-9782
Fax: 806-792-9785

McAllen Vet Center
801 Nolana Loop Suite 140
McAllen, TX 78504
Phone: 956-631-2147
Fax: 956-631-2430

Midland Vet Center
2817 W. Loop 250 N., Suite E
Midland, TX 79707
Phone: 432-697-8222
Fax: 432-697-0561

Tarrant County Vet Center
3337 W. Pioneer Pkwy, Northlake Center
Pantego, TX 76013
Phone: 817-274-0981
Fax: 817-274-9712

San Antonio Vet Center
231 W. Cypress St. Suite 100
San Antonio, TX 78212
Phone: 210-472-4025
Fax: 210-472-4032

Utah

Provo Vet Center
1807 No. 1120 West
Provo, UT 84604
Phone: 801-377-1117
Fax: 801-377-0227

Salt Lake Vet Center
1354 East 3300 South
Salt Lake, UT 84106
Phone: 801-584-1294
Fax: 801-487-6243

Vermont

South Burlington Vet Center
359 Dorset St.
South Burlington, VT 05403
Phone: 802-862-1806
Fax: 802-865-3319

White River Junction Vet Center
Gilman Office, Building #2, 222 Holiday Inn Drive
White River Junction, VT 05001
Phone: 802-295-2908
Fax: 802-296-3653

Virginia

Alexandria Vet Center
6940 South Kings Highway #204
Alexandria, VA 22310
Phone: 703-360-8633
Fax: 703-360-2935

Norfolk Vet Center
1711 Church Street, Suites A&B
Norfolk, VA 23504
Phone: 757-623-7584
Fax: 757-441-6621

Richmond Vet Center
4902 Fitzhugh Avenue
Richmond, VA 23230
Phone: 804-353-8958
Fax: 804-353-0837

Roanoke Vet Center
350 Albemarle Ave., SW
Roanoke, VA 24016
Phone: 540-342-9726
Fax: 540-857-2405

Virginia Beach County Vet Center
324 Southport Circle, Suite 102
Virginia Beach, VA 23452
Phone: 757-248-3665
Fax: 757-248-3667

Washington

Bellingham Vet Center
3800 Byron Ave Suite 124
Bellingham, WA 98229
Phone: 360-733-9226
Fax: 360-733-9117

Everett Vet Center
3311 Wetmore Avenue
Everett, WA 98201
Phone: 425-252-9701
Fax: 425-252-9728

Federal Way Vet Center
32020 32nd Ave South Suite 110
Federal Way, WA 98001
Phone: 253-838-3090

Seattle Vet Center
2030 - 9th Ave. Suite 210
Seattle, WA 98121
Phone: 206-553-2706
Fax: 206-553-0380

Spokane Vet Center
100 No. Mullan Rd., Suite 102
Spokane, WA 99206
Phone: 509-444-8387
Fax: 509-444-8388

Tacoma Vet Center
4916 Center St. Suite E
Tacoma, WA 98409
Phone: 253-565-7038
Fax: 253-565-4981

Yakima Valley Vet Center
2119 West Lincoln Avenue
Yakima, WA 98902
Phone: 509-457-2736
Fax: 509-457-1822

West Virginia

Beckley Vet Center
1000 Johnstown Road
Beckley, WV 25801
Phone: 304-252-8220
Fax: 304-254-8711

Charleston Vet Center
521 Central Avenue
Charleston, WV 25302
Phone: 304-343-3825
Fax: 304-347-5303

Logan, West Virginia Vet Center Outstation
21 Veterans Avenue
Henlawson, WV 25624
Phone: 304-752-4453
Fax: 304-752-6910

Huntington Vet Center
3135 16th Street Road Suite 11
Huntington, WV 25701
Phone: 304-523-8387
Fax: 304-529-5910

Martinsburg Vet Center
900 Winchester Avenue
Martinburg, WV 25401
Phone: 304-263-6776
Fax: 304-262-7448

Morgantown Vet Center
1083 Greenbag Road
Morgantown, WV 26508
Phone: 304-291-4303
Fax: 304-291-4251

Parkersburg Vet Center Outstation
2311 Ohio Avenue, Suite D
Pakersburg, WV 26101
Phone: 304-485-1599
Fax: 304-485-4212
Toll Free: 1-800-591-6001

Princeton Vet Center
905 Mercer Street
Princeton, WV 24740
Phone: 304-425-5653
Fax: 304-425-2837

Wheeling Vet Center
1206 Chapline Street
Wheeling, WV 26003
Phone: 304-232-0587
Fax: 304-232-1031

Wisconsin

Green Bay Vet Center
1600 S. Ashland Ave
Green Bay, WI 54304
Phone: 920-435-5650
Fax: 920-435-5086

La Crosse Vet Center
20 Copeland Ave.
La Crosse, WI 54601
Phone: 608-782-4403
Fax: 608-782-4423

Madison Vet Center
706 Williamson Street
Madison, WI 53703
Phone: 608-264-5342
Fax: 608-264-5344

Milwaukee Vet Center
5401 N. 76th St.
Milwaukee, WI 53218
Phone: 414-536-1301
Fax: 414-536-1568

Wyoming

Casper Vet Center (Satellite)
1030 North Poplar Suite B
Casper, WY 82601
Phone: 307-261-5355
Fax: 307-261-5439

Cheyenne Vet Center
3219 E Pershing Blvd
Cheyenne, WY 82001
Phone: 307-778-7370
Fax: 307-638-8923

American Samoa

American Samoa Vet Center
Ottoville Road
Pago Pago, AS 96799

Mailing Address:
P.O. Box 982942
Pago Pago, AS 96799
Phone: 684-258-7254
Fax: 684-699-3731

Guam

Guam Vet Center
222 Chalan Santo Papa Reflection Ctr. Ste 201
Hagatna, GU 96910
Phone: 671-472-7160
Fax: 671-472-7162

Puerto Rico

Arecibo Vet Center
50 Gonzalo Marin St
Arecibo, PR 612
Phone: 787-879-4510
Fax: 787-879-4944

Ponce Vet Center
35 Mayor St. Suite 1
Ponce, PR 730
Phone: 787-841-3260
Fax: 787-841-3165

San Juan Vet Center
Cond. Medical Center Plaza Suite
LC 8, 9 & 11, Urb. La Riviera
Rio Piedras, PR 0921
Phone: 787-749-4409
Fax: 787-749-4416

Virgin Islands

St. Croix Vet Center Satellite
The Village Mall, RR 2 Box 10553 Kingshill
St. Croix, VI 0850
Phone: 340-778-5553
Fax: 340-778-5545

St. Thomas Vet Center Satellite
Buccaneer Mall, Suite #8
St. Thomas, VI 0802
Phone: 340-774-6674
Fax: 340-774-5384

EDITOR'S NOTE

I suppose it's horribly cliché of me to say I had a complicated relationship with my father, but really, I did. We were, in many ways, far too alike, and it showed up worst when we were at odds. Each of us had a unique texture of stubbornness, and when we collided, it was like flint and steel, complete with shooting sparks and flaring tempers. It didn't help that he was sometimes a very heavy drinker, which served to draw out his demons. As a result, I heard about things growing up that were at once too horrific for me to understand and, based on what I could figure out, too haunting to forget. He spoke often of all those he lost in the conflict over in Vietnam, and I think he must have been racked with survivor's guilt, especially since he was only ten minutes away from getting on the plane to go over there when his Army Reserve unit was recalled stateside. My dad used to say that if not for that last minute change of orders, I might not even be here due to the timing of my conception.

My father's drunken lectures often lasted for hours, each topic more traumatizing than the last and expanding to include other wars. Because of all I grew up hearing about—the torture of POWs, the Bataan Death March, the scandal at the Hanoi Hilton, the missing limbs, the crying families, the blood—I came to internally cringe whenever the word "veteran" was spoken around me. I would purposefully turn off the news, click away from websites, or quietly sidle away from conversations whenever the topic came up. For years, I hoped those avoidance practices would keep me from having to face my father's demons, even though they had already dug their claws in me through his stories. And then, at the age of 38, I unknowingly became friends with a vet.

I met Dave Kashmer through another friend, one who lives near me in Colorado. Both men grew up in Syracuse, New York, where Dave still lives today. I have only met Dave once in person, but he became a good friend on Facebook. In early 2011, he told me that he'd found a page on Facebook dedicated to military personnel with PTSD and their families. He knew I had civilian PTSD and thought I might find some solace for myself in that community. This was the first time he'd mentioned his military background, and when I saw how many vets were visiting the page, I was quick to click away as usual. I expressed, truthfully, that I was happy Dave was finding the help he needed, but I didn't think there was anything for me to be found there.

Two weeks later, I got another message from Dave. The woman who ran the page, Shawn, was struggling with editors over her book because she employed an unorthodox method of writing. She spoke her words into a computer that would then produce a written transcription. The end result was a text that read like she spoke, which was turning out to be a big issue with the editors to whom she had already submitted. Dave asked me if I would take a look at her blog that had a small sampling of the first part of her book. I did, and though some of her work came across a little colloquial, I heard a real Voice in her words and thought her to be a good storyteller. I told Dave Shawn's blog was excellent compared to other blogs but the style was unusual enough that I could understand why a lot of editors wouldn't know quite what to make of it.

After more of Dave's urging, I agreed to email Shawn with my editor's perspective on her work, and as I usually do, I put my phone number at the end of my message and told her she could call me if she had any questions. She called that very afternoon. I listened as she expressed her passion about her need to protect and deliver her own Voice. Thus far she hadn't found the right match in an editor. So, she was a heartbeat away from self-publishing through either Amazon.com or Ingram Lightning Source, but she was about to tear out her hair from all the technical processes involved. At that point, I decided to step into the light and reveal myself to be not only an editor, but also an editor with my own publishing house.

That phone call was on March 23. I am writing this note very early on the morning of July 26. Like so many other nights between then and now, I've had no sleep, and I've only taken a couple of days off from the business of getting Shawn's book edited and ready for press. Early on we chose September 11, 2011 as the launch date for the book, knowing that to fit in all the work that needed to be done would be almost impossibly tight. We were driven by the knowledge that it would be so worth it to get The War at Home out there as soon as possible. As part of "auditioning" for the role of Shawn's publisher, I joined her Facebook page and, later, her Facebook group. I got to know the people in that community pretty quickly. Their stories gripped me. They all had one element in common: deep pain. Whether vet or spouse or close caregiver, everyone was fighting emotional and sometimes physical battles on a daily basis even though they were not in combat zones anymore, even though the fighting should have been over. I felt so moved that I chose to take on the impossible: to push Shawn's book through the publication process in time to launch on our chosen day. I felt like it was the least I could do.

Through most of the work on this book, my focus was on what I could give to the project: my editing expertise, my company's resources for printing and distribution, and my nigh-on endless supplies of energy and encouragement. I had no idea I would wind up gaining so much myself. For starters, I gained a strong friendship and professional relationship with Shawn. We think very much alike, but her area of expertise is in marketing, which is one of my blind spots. I'm happy to say that we've ended up hiring her on as our official Marketing Guru. There's also the fact that her book stands to be our best-selling title starting on the first day of sales. That certainly will help us expand our company! But the biggest surprise comes in the form of a huge emotional payoff that I never saw coming: An improved understanding of my father and a deeper connection to him.

Now, my father actually passed on about 18 years ago. In the last 2 years of his life, he quit drinking and became more of a person to whom I could connect. Our last conversation was on the night before he died, though neither one of us knew it would be the last. I thought we had shared and settled every aspect of our complicated relationship that night. He told me he was proud of me, that he loved me, and that he wanted me to do something with my writing, which was something he'd never endorsed before. But now I realize that his passion about the way veterans were mistreated and misunderstood was not something we ever really spoke about in his last years. When he stopped drinking, he also stopped talking about all that.

After spending 4 very intense months eating, sleeping, and breathing the issues affecting veterans with PTSD, I finally get it. My father was so dismayed, disgusted, frustrated, and angry that it wasn't something he could talk about when sober. I understand this because this is how I feel now (minus the getting drunk part). I have very complex feelings about war and violence, tending to follow more of a pacifist line of thinking than most around me, but my attitudes about the way veterans are treated is now very clear. What I've seen has shown me that, just as it did in my father's day, our military system is taking in these young people, chewing them up, and spitting them out. They are every bit as much victims of the combat as anyone else caught up in these conflicts. Most of them were just trying to find some kind of career that would help them progress in life. Instead, many of them have become fractured people living shattered lives. The stories of loss are just heartbreaking—divorce, homelessness, unemployment, chemical dependency (including prescriptions), and attempted suicide. They deserve better. My father knew it, and so do I.

I don't know where this journey will lead next. I've met so many people through Shawn, some of whom are already lined up to publish their own stories through our company. And I have an intuition that this is just the beginning. Something I do know for sure is that I will always be grateful to Dave who led me to Shawn and to Shawn herself for helping me hear what I couldn't before: My heartbeat is an echo of the one that thumped in my dad.

~~ Spring Lea Henry, Editor

COMMUNICATIONS WORKSHEETS FOR VETERANS AND THEIR SPOUSES

Worksheet for Couples Communication

This is for use by both spouses, especially when there is a disagreement.

What happened today?

Why was the vet so angry?

Did I accuse?

Could I have reached out more?

Could I have worded things differently?

Did I hear what my spouse was saying?

Did I make sure my spouse understood what I was saying?

How do I feel now?

Could I have handled anything differently?

Worksheet for Veteran's Stress

This is for use by the veteran to help think through PTSD incidents.

What happened?

How did you feel?

What triggered you?

Has this triggered you before?

Did it remind you of something?

Did you have a flashback?

Did you get startled?

Did you smell, hear, or see something that reminded you of a trauma incident?

Looking back could you have controlled your anger better?

Are you reacting before thinking?

Did you talk to anyone about this?

Decision-Making Worksheet

This is for both spouses who feel unhappy with aspects of their relationship.

With any situation that makes one unhappy, there are three healthy choices for a solution:

1. Leave the situation.
2. Change the situation.
3. Stay in the situation without whining and complaining.

Any one of the three could be a way to make things better. Continuing to complain about the same problems over and over does not change anything and is, therefore, unproductive.

What is the situation making me unhappy?

Decision-Making Worksheet (cont.)

1. If I were to leave the situation, what would that look like? Would that require me to change my thinking, create some sort of physical separation, or take a time-out? Leaving a situation doesn't necessarily mean leaving your spouse, but sometimes it does.

2. If I were to change the situation, knowing that it is only possible to change what lies within me and not change what is in my spouse, what would I do to make a difference? Could I change the way I speak, alter my daily routines, or consult outside help?

3. If I am to stay without complaint, what must I do to change my thinking so that this is a tolerable situation? Can I work on not taking things personally? Can I change the way I view and speak about the situation to highlight what is working instead of what isn't? Can I envision a day when the situation might change and go forward knowing this is only a temporary discomfort?

NOTES

COLOPHON

The original source for this book was created in Scribus on a Dell Mini running the Ubutu Linux operating system and output as PDF.

The fonts used in this book are Bradley Hand ITC, CrackHouse, FreeSans, Merri Christina, Times New Roman, URW Bookman L.

The book was printed "on-demand" by Lightning Source, Inc. on creme paper and perfect-bound.

Pages: 320

Book designer: Ray Henry

Cover designer: Rose L. Hayden

Cover photo: Andrew Grammer

Editor: Spring Lea Henry

Additional designers: Shawn J. Gourley

For other credits see page iv

For legal notices see pages iv to vi

If You Enjoyed This Book, You May Also Like:

CPSIA information can be obtained at www.ICGtesting.com
Printed in the USA
LVOW061356211211

260510LV00003B/23/P

9 780979 008467